Pompeii
Timbuktu
ROME
BALTIC
Madison
You Are Here.

The Best Pet Name Book Ever

SM

4th ed.

BARRON'S

4th Edition

Wayne Bryant Eldridge, DVM

About the Author

Dr. Wayne Bryant Eldridge is a veterinarian, as well as founder of Eldridge Animal Hospital, Pets First Veterinary Center, The Pet Place Veterinary Center, and Access Veterinary Care in San Antonio, Texas, where he has practiced his profession for over 30 years.

He earned his undergraduate degree and a Doctor of Veterinary Medicine from Texas A&M University in 1971.

Dr. Eldridge is an author and speaker on various topics pertaining to veterinary medicine and pets. His areas of special interest include animal behavior and the human-animal bond.

Acknowledgments

I am grateful to my parents, Adelene and Jack Eldridge, for their continual faith in me throughout the years. Thanks to my children, Lori Eldridge Osborn and Wayne Bryant Eldridge, Jr., for their love and encouragement.

Also, Darrell Buono, Caitlin Sweeny, and the staff at Barron's are to be commended for their work to make this book a reality.

All inquiries should be addressed to:
Barron's Educational Series, Inc.
250 Wireless Boulevard
Hauppauge, New York 11788
www.barronseduc.com

ISBN-13: 978-0-7641-4416-5
ISBN-10: 0-7641-4416-2

Library of Congress Catalog Card No. 2009050837

Library of Congress Cataloging-in-Publication Data
Eldridge, Wayne Bryant.
    The best pet name book ever! / Wayne Bryant Eldridge — 4th ed.
        p.   cm.
    ISBN-13: 978-0-7641-4416-5
    ISBN-10: 0-7641-4416-2
    1. Pets—Names. I. Title.
SF411.3.E43   2010
929.9'7—dc22   2009050837

PRINTED IN THE UNITED STATES OF AMERICA

9 8 7 6 5 4 3 2 1

DEDICATION

This book is dedicated to all caring pet owners and
to the celebration of the human-animal bond.

Contents

Introduction

During my thirty years as a practicing veterinarian, many of the pets brought to me for their first examinations have had no names—not because of apathy on the owner's part but because of the lack of a guide in the name selection process; thus, the owners of these pets sometimes ask for my suggestions. The thousands of requests that I have received originally prompted me to compile a list of unusual pet names; later, I categorized the growing list according to general subject areas, such as historical names and names of foods. This method of categorization has helped hundreds of my clients choose names—not just any name, but a unique one—for their pets. Consequently, I have decided to organize my categories into a book so that I can assist a wider range of pet owners.

The Best Pet Name Book Ever is a creative guide for naming those special animals in our lives. Some of the names in this book are actual names of my patients taken from the files of my animal hospital; others come from interviews with pet owners; and the remainder results from research into the various categories into which I have classified the names. This book seeks to give you an overview of examples of pet names (in particular, those for dogs and cats, but not exclusively), and by no means constitutes a complete list, because as I've learned, the possibilities are limitless. You should use *The Best Pet Name Book Ever,* then, not as the comprehensive source on this subject, but rather as a tool to spark your imagination.

When choosing one of the names from this book or one of your own invention, you should keep in mind a couple of helpful hints. First, pick a name that your pet can easily recognize. Cats and dogs respond better to one and two syllable words: "Ezekiel" is a creative choice; however, your cat will respond more readily to the shortened "Ziggy" or "Zeke." Also, avoid giving your dog a name that sounds like one of the basic commands ("No," "Down," "Sit," "Stay," "Come," etc.). A dog named "Star" may have difficulty distinguishing her name from "Stay." Nevertheless, do not let these considerations restrict your creativity.

"How about…" At the beginning of each chapter, you will find a list of unique or noteable suggestions from the list that follows. This might help you narrow down your choices if you are having trouble deciding.

Note: If another name within the same chapter appears in the body of an entry, SMALL CAPITALS make reference to that name—for example:

Cyprus   The island where APHRODITE was born.

"Pretty Boy"

Appearance

The most obvious and simple way to name your pet is by its appearance. This basis for choosing a name works especially well for a new pet whose personality and peculiarities have not yet revealed themselves to you. However, keep in mind that as a pet ages, its appearance may change and the name you originally chose for your animal may no longer apply. For example, "Fur Ball" is a cute name for a kitten, but it may not suit a fully grown tomcat. Still, such a situation where the name may become inappropriate rarely occurs, and basing a pet's name on its appearance can result in a fascinating and appropriate name.

How About . . .

Bandit

Bear

Bitsy

Cutie

Midnight

Mittens

Oreo

Shaggy

Snowball

Appearance

Adobe
Agate
Albino
Amber
Ashes
Baby Bear
Baby Boy
Baby Doll
Baby Girl
Baby Kitty
Badger
Bandit
Bat Cat
Bear
Beige-ing
Big 'n
Big Boy
Big Foot
Big One
Big Paw
Big Red
Biscuit
Bits
Bitsie
Bitsy

Black
Black Ace
Black Cat
Black Jack
Blackberry
Blackie
Blacky
Blanca
Blanco
Blanquita
Blinker
Blondie
Blue
Bob Cat
Boots
Bootsie
Boxcar
Brandy
Bright Eyes
Brillo
Britches
Brown Spots
Brownie
Browny
Buffey

Buffie
Buffy
Bunny
Bushy
Butter Fingers
Button
Buttons
Cali
Calico
Calley
Camo
 (Camouflage)
Caracal
Carbon
Carmel
Caspar

Chalk Paw
Charcoal
Charmin
Checkers
Chiquita
Chocolate
Chops
Chubbs
Chubby
Cinder
Cinnamon
Clay
Cobalt
Coal
Coco
Coco Bear

HEARTBREAKERS . . .	
Blondie	Foxy Lady
Bright Eyes	Ginger
Chiquita	Honey
Cinnamon	Miss Pretty
Cutie	Slim

Cocoa	Dusty	Fuzz Ball	Jaguar
Cookie	Ebony	Fuzzy	Jaguarundi
Copper	Eclipse	Genius	Jumbo
Cotton	Eight Ball	Ghost	Kaffir
Cottonball	Ember	Ginger	Khaki
Cottontail	Fancy	Ginger Snap	Kong
Coyote	Fang	Gold Cat	Lefty
Crackers	Fat Boy	Goldie	Leo
Cream	Fat Cat	Gray	Licorice
Crimson	Fatso	Gray Bear	Lilly White
Crystal	Fawn	Gray Cat	Limpy
Cue Ball	Feather(s)	Gray Spots	Lion
Curlie	Flame	Hairy	Little
Curly	Flaps	Half Pint	Little One
Curry	Floppy	Hershey	Lobo
Cutie	Flopsy	Hi-Ho Silver	Locket
Daffy	Fluffy	Hobbles	Longfellow
Daylight	Four Paws	Hog	(a dachshund)
Diamond	Foxie	Honey	Lumpy
Dinky	Foxy Lady	Hot Dog	Lynx
Dog	Freckles	Hulk	Mama Cat
Doll	Frostie	Husky	Mama Kitty
Domino	Frosty	Inky	Manly
Droopy	Fudge	Iota	Manx
Dust Mop	Funny Face	Ivory	Many Paws

Appearance

Mauve	Mud	Panther	Porker
Midget	Muffin	Patches	Porky
Midnight	Munchkin	Paws	Powder
Minnie Paws	Nugget	Pee Wee	Pretty Boy
Miss Pretty	Nutmeg	Pepper	Pretty Girl
Mitten(s)	Ocelot	Perky	Pudgy
Momma Cat	Onyx	Phantom	Puff
Momma Dog	Orange Kitty	Pig	Puff Ball
Moose	Oreo	Piglet	Puffy
Mother Cat	Oso	Pink Kitty	Pug
Mouse	Panda	Pinky	Puma

"Porky"

Pumpkin	Sherman (tank)	Speckles	Tiptoe
Pygmy	Shinola	Splotch	Tomcat
Quad Pod	Shorty	Spot(s)	Toothpick
Q Ball	Sienna	Spotty	Toy
Rags	Silky	Squat	Tramp
Rainbow	Slick (a snake)	Squint	Trinket
Raven	Slim	Squirt	Tubs
Red	Slinky	Stash (moustache)	Tux
Runt	Smidgen	Stretch	Twiggy
Rusty	Smokey	Stripe(s)	Twinkles
Sable	Smudge	Striper	Ugly (Ug)
Sage	Sneakers	Stripie	Velcro
Sandy	Snow	Swirl	Velvet
Satin	Snow Bear	Tabby	Weenie Dog
Sausage Dog	Snowball	Tar Baby	Weiner Dog
Scottie	Snowflake	Target	Whale
Scrawny	Snowman	Tawny	Whiskers
Scruffy	Snowshoes	Ten	Whitey
Seis (Six-toed cat)	Snowy	Tiger	Whitie
Serval	Socks	Tiny	Wildcat
Shadow	Spade	Tip	Wolf
Shaggy	Sparkle(s)	Tippy	Yellow

"Happy Cat"

Personality

Personality, like appearance, is one of the most obvious characteristics upon which to base a pet's name. However, as I mentioned in Chapter 1, a new pet's personality may not fully emerge at first and may change as a pet grows older. While it is important to remember these considerations when choosing your pet's name, a name derived from a dominant personality trait will usually prove appropriate through-out your pet's life.

How About . . .

Angel	Jet
Chuckles	Nibbles
Frisky	Ranger
Goofy	Scooter
Grumpy	Sniffles

Personality

Amble	Banshee	Candy	Comet
Angel	Barky	Caracal	Cool
Anxious	Bear	Chainsaw	Couch Potato
Apathy	Blinky	Chance	Country
Attack	Blitz	Chancy	Coyote
Baby Bear	Blue	Chaos	Cozy
Baby Kitty	Bomber	Charmer	Crash
Back Talk	Bonkers	Chase	Crazy
Bad Cat	Browser	Chatterbox	Crunch
Badger	Bruiser	Chewie	Cuddles
Ballerina	Bubba Fat	Chewy	Cujo
Bandit	Bully	Chuckles	Cutter

"Chuckles"

Daffy	Flash	Grumpy	Jinx
Dancer	Flip	Gunner	Joe Cool
Dandy	Flounder	Gypsy	Jumper
Dash	Fox	Ham	Kaffir
Demon	Foxy	Happy	Killer
Dennis the Menace	Fraidy Cat	Happy Cat	Kinky
	Freaky	Hiccup	Kissy
Digger	Freeloader	Highball	Kitty Witty
Ding-a-ling	Friendly	Hobo	Lady
Dingbat	Friskie	Hokey	Lefty
Dingy	Frisky	Honey	Leo
Dirtball	Front Porch Cat	Hoover	Licker
Dodger	Fruity	Hot Dog	Licky
Dr. Jekyll	Fury	Howler	Lightnin'
Dracula	Gabby	Hugger	Lion
Duster	Genius	Hunter	Loner
Fearless	Ginger Snapper	Ice	Lonesome
Feisty	Goofus	Impulse	Looney
Fighter	Goofy	Itchy	Lover
Finesse	Goony	Jaguar	Lover Boy
Finicky	Grabber	Jaguarundi	Lover Girl
Flake	Gremlin	Jaws	Lovey
Flakey	Groovy	Jet	Lucky

Personality

Lynx	Nibbles	Rambler	Shadow
Magic	Nightmare	Ranger	Shady
Mama Trouble	Noble	Rascal	Sharp
Manly	Nocturne	Rebel	Shock
Mate	Nosey	Rogue	Shocker
Meathead	Ocelot	Rough	Shredder
Meow	Oddball	Rover	Sir Lick-a-Lot
Mew	Pampas	Rowdy	Sissy
Mew-Mew	Peepers	Ruckus	Skamp
Mickey Mouth	Peppy	Rumble	Skamper
Mischief	Pistol	Runner	Skidatel
Miss Piggy	Play Kitty	Sassy	Sleazy
Miss Priss	Pliers	Saucy	Sleek
Miss Sassy	Pokey	Scamp	Sleepy
Monkey	Pompous	Scarlet	Slipper
Moody	Prancer	Schitzo	Slow Poke
Mop	Prissy	Scooter	Slumber
Motor	Puddles	Scout	Sly
Mouser	Puma	Scrapper	Smooch
Moxy	Punch	Scrappy	Snapback
Mr. Hyde	Pushy	Scratches	Snapper
Nervous Ninny	Quick	Screwball	Snappy
Nibbler	Radar	Serval	Sneaky

Sneezy	Squeaky	Tramp	Watchcat
Sniffer	Squiggles	Trip	Watchdog
Sniffles	Sticker	Tripper	Weasel
Sniffy	Stinky	Trooper	Weedeater
Snoopy	Stray	Trotter	Wicked
Snooze	Stray Cat	Troubles	Wiggles
Snoozer	Swishie	Trusty	Wild Thing
Snuggler	Taffy	Tuffy	Wildcat
Snuggles	Tag	Tugger	Winker
Solo	Teaser	Turbo	Winky
Spacey	Teddy Bear	Useless	Witty Kitty
Speedy	Terminator	Vagrant	Woofer
Spinner	Thumper	Valiant	Worm
Spirit	Tiger	Vampire	Worthless
Splash	Tom	Vanity	
Spooky	Tough Cat	Wags	
Spunky	Tracker	Warrior	

"Jacques"

Human Names

A pet with a human name tends to have a special relationship with its owner, who often regards the pet as a surrogate child or best friend. In fact, many owners name their pets after a person they have known, a relative, or someone they admire. Frequently, a human name can best depict the character, or nature, of a pet; for instance, "Reginald" vividly suggests the qualities of a basset hound. Likewise, a pet may resemble—hopefully not to a great extent—someone you know. If you can name your pet after this person without offending him or her, then you have further established your pet's unique identity.

How About . . .

Abigail	Joshua
Ava	Isabella
Bessie	Madison
Bradford	Oscar
Buddy	Owen
Ginger	Rich

Human Names

Aaron	Allie	Arnold	Bentley
Abby	Allison	Arthur	Bernard
Abe	Amanda	Ashleigh	Bernie
Abigail	Amando	Ashley	Bert
Adam	Amelia	Audrey	Bertha
Adelene	Amos	Ava	Bessie
Adolph	Amy	Babette	Beth
Adrian	Andre	Bailey	Betsy
Adriana	Andrea	Barbie	Bianca
Agatha	Andrew	Barkley	Bill
Agnes	Andy	Barnaby	Billie
Al	Angela	Barney	Billy
Alan	Ann	Barnie	Billy Bob
Albert	Anna	Barry	Blaire
Alec	Anne	Bart	Bobbi
Alex	Annette	Bartholomew	Bobby
Alexander	Annie	Basil	Bonnie
Alfred	Anthony	Bea	Boris
Alice	April	Beau	Bosley
Alisa	Arby	Becky	Brad
Alison	Archie	Belle	Bradford
Allan	Armstrong	Ben	Bradley
Allen	Arnie	Benji	Brady

Brando	Burt	Charley	Clem
Brandon	Buford	Charlie	Clementine
Brandy	Byron	Charlotte	Cleo
Brent	Calvin	Chaz	Cliff
Brett	Cammie	Chelsea	Clifford
Brewster	Cammy	Cher	Clint
Brian	Candice	Cheryl	Clinton
Bridget	Carley	Chester	Cody
Bridgette	Carlos	Chet	Colby
Britt	Carmella	Chris	Colette
Brittany	Carmen	Christina	Colleen
Brooke	Carol	Christopher	Colline
Brooks	Casey	Chuck	Connie
Bruce	Casper	Chuckie	Corey
Bruno	Cassidy	Ciel	Courtney
Brutus	Cassie	Cindy	Craig
Bryan	Caterina	Clancy	Crystal
Bryant	Catherine	Clancey	Curt
Bubba	Cathy	Clara	Curtis
Bubba Smith	Catrina	Clare	Cynthia
Buck	Cecil	Clark	Daisy
Bud	Celia	Claudia	Dale
Buddy	Charles	Clay	Damon

Human Names

Dan	Dolly	Edy	Evette
Dana	Dominic	Elaine	Ezra
Daniel	Dominique	Eli	Faith
Daniella	Don	Elisabeth	Fannie
Danielle	Donald	Elizabeth	Fay
Danny	Donna	Ellen	Felicia
Daphne	Donnie	Ellie	Felix
Darcy	Dory	Elliot	Fergie
Darren	Dot	Elmer	Fletch
David	Dottie	Elsa	Flo
Davy	Doug	Elsie	Floyd
Dawn	Douglas	Elvira	Foster
Debbie	Drew	Emilio	Fran
Dee	Dudley	Emily	Francine
Dennis	Duncan	Emma	Francis
Derek	Dustin	Eric	Frank
Derrick	Dwayne	Erik	Frankie
Devan	Dylan	Erin	Frannie
Dexter	Earl	Ernest	Fred
Diana	Edgar	Ethan	Freddie
Dodie	Edie	Eunice	Freddy
Dody	Edward	Eva	Frederick
Dollie	Edwin	Evan	Gabby

Gary	Gunther	Howard	Jasper
Gayle	Gussie	Huey	Jean
Gene	Gwen	Ian	Jedgar
George	Hailey	Igor	Jeffrey
Georgette	Haley	Ilsa	Jen
Georgia	Hannah	Inga	Jenna
Gerard	Hans	Ingrid	Jennie
Gerrie	Harold	Ira	Jennifer
Gertie	Harry	Irving	Jenny
Gertrude	Harv	Isa	Jeremy
Gina	Harvey	Isabella	Jerry
Ginger	Hattie	Ivan	Jess
Ginnie	Hazel	Jack	Jesse
Ginny	Heather	Jackie	Jessica
Gloria	Helen	Jacob	Jessie
Golda	Henry	Jacques	Jezabel
Grace	Herbie	Jake	Jill
Gracey	Herman	James	Jim
Gracie	Hilary	Jamie	Jimmie
Greg	Hilda	Jan	Jimmy
Greta	Hogan	Jane	Joan
Gretchen	Hollis	Janie	Joann
Guido	Holly	Jason	Joanne

Human Names

Jock	Judy	Kristen	Linda
Jodie	Jules	Kristie	Lindsay
Jody	Julia	Kristy	Lisa
Joe	Julie	Lacey	Liz
Joel	Julius	Lacie	Liza
Joela	Justin	Lance	Lizzy
Joey	Karen	Lanna	Lois
John	Kate	Larry	Lola
John Alex	Katelyn	Laura	Lolita
John Henry	Katherine	Lauren	Lollie
Johnny	Kathryn	Lea	Lora
Jonathan	Kathy	Leanne	Loren
Jones	Katie	Lee	Lori
Joni	Katy	Leland	Lottie
Jonie	Kay	Lena	Lou
Jordan	Kelly	Leroy	Louie
Joseph	Kent	Lesley	Louis
Josephine	Kerry	Leslie	Louise
Josh	Kevin	Lester	Lucas
Joshua	Kim	Lianna	Lucy
Josie	Kimberly	Libby	Luigi
Joya	Kimbrey	Lilli	Luke
Joyce	Kit	Lilly	Mabel

Mable	Martha	Michael	Nancy
Maddy	Martin	Michelle	Naomi
Madeline	Marvin	Mickey	Natalie
Madison	Mathilda	Mike	Nathan
Maggie	Matt	Mikey	Ned
Magnum	Matthew	Miles	Neil
Malcolm	Mattie	Millie	Nell
Mandy	Maude	Mindy	Nellie
Mangus	Maudie	Mira	Nelly
Marcey	Maureen	Miriam	Newt
Marcia	Maven	Missy	Nicholas
Marcie	Mavis	Misty	Nick
Marcus	Max	Mitch	Nicky
Marge	Maxine	Molly	Nicole
Margie	May	Monique	Niki
Margo	Maynard	Montgomery	Noel
Maria	McGee	Monty	Nora
Marianne	Meagan	Morris	Norman
Marie	Meg	Muriel	Olin
Mark	Megan	Murphy	Olivia
Marlene	Melissa	Murray	Olive
Marsha	Melvin	Nadine	Oliver
Marshie	Mia	Nance	Ollie

Human Names

Oscar	Phyllis	Rita	Samantha
Otto	Polly	Robert	Sammy
Owen	Pollyanna	Robin	Sandy
Pam	Priscilla	Roger	Sara
Pamela	Prudy	Ron	Sarah
Panchito	Rachel	Ronald	Sasha
Pancho	Ralph	Ronney	Saul
Parker	Randolph	Ronnie	Schroder
Patrick	Randy	Roscoe	Schultz
Patty	Raquel	Rose	Scott
Paula	Raymond	Roxanne	Scottie
Pearl	Reba	Roy	Sean
Peg	Rebecca	Rudy	Sebastian
Penelope	Reginald	Russ	Seth
Percival	Rene	Russell	Seymour
Percy	Renee	Rusty	Shannon
Pete	Rex	Ruth	Sharon
Petey	Rhett	Ryan	Shawn
Petra	Rich	Sabre	Shayne
Petula	Richard	Sabrina	Sheila
Phil	Rick	Sadie	Shelby
Philip	Ricky	Sally	Shelly
Phoebe	Riley	Sam	Sherry

Shirley	Tamara	Tommy	Wally
Sibyl	Tammy	Tony	Walter
Sid	Tanya	Tracy	Warren
Sidney	Taylor	Travis	Wayne
Sophie	Ted	Trenton	Webster
Stacey	Teddy	Trevor	Wendy
Stanley	Teena	Trish	Wilbur
Stella	Templeton	Trudy	William
Stephanie	Teresa	Tucker	Willie
Stephen	Teri	Tyler	Willy
Steven	Tessi	Valerie	Wilma
Stuart	Tessie	Van	Windy
Sue	Theodore	Vanessa	Winnie
Susan	Thomas	Vaughan	Winston
Susie	Tiffany	Vera	Woodrow
Susy	Timmy	Vic	Wylie
Suzanne	Timothy	Vick	Yvette
Suzette	Tina	Vicky	Yvonne
Suzie	Toby	Victor	Zachary
Suzy	Todd	Vincent	Zane
Sylvia	Toddy	Virgil	Zeke
Tabitha	Tom	Virginia	Zoe

"Honey Bunny"

BROCCOLI

Terms of Endearment

Many people use terms of endearment to refer to members of their families. A large number of people also use such terms when addressing their pets. Names such as "Baby" and "Sweetie" may not have originally been a dog's or cat's name, but through repeated use, an owner may come to refer to his or her pet in that manner. Many owners, however, choose a term of endearment for a special pet's name right away, and these names are often nearest and dearest to his or her heart.

How About . . .

Bubba

Honey

Junior

Love

Marshmallow

Puddin'

Sugar Pie

Sweet Pea

Tootsie

Terms of Endearment

Ace	Fifi	Kissy Bear	Punkin
Angel	Fluffer	Kissy Face	Purdy
Babe	Fu Fu	Kitter	Sugar
Baby	Fuffy	Lad	Sugar 'n Spice
Baby Bear	Gin Gin	Laddie	Sugar Baby
Baby Cakes	Ginger Sugar	Lov-a-Lot	Sugar Bear
Baby Doll	Gingi Girl	Love	Sugar Pie
Baby Girl	Girly	Lover Boy	Sugar Plum
Baby Kitty	Good Boy	Lover Girl	Sugarfoot
Beau Beau	Good Girl	Lovey	Sugarkins
Bitsie	Hey Girl	Lovey Lou	Sunshine
Bitsy	Honey	Lovums	Suzie Q
Bubba	Honey Blue	Marshmallow	Sweet Pea
Bubby	Honey Bunny	Nuffin	Sweet Thing
Buffer	Honey Dew	Pal	Sweetie
Cutsie	Hot Dog	Patty Cake	Sweetie Pie
Cutie Pie	Hotlips	Precious	Sweetums
Dickens	Itsy-Bitsy	Pudden	Tootsie
Duster	Junior	Puddin'	True Blue
Dusty	Keeper	Puddy Tat	

"Marshmallow"

"Washington"

Historical Names

Many owners choose historical names for their pets, either because they enjoy history, because a particular historical figure interests them, or a pet actually resembles a well-known character from history. For instance, the name "Napoleon Bonaparte" could accurately describe a small, feisty dog. This chapter contains the names of some famous—and some infamous—dogs and cats of the past and a sampling of the names of the prominent figures of world history. The list of the latter is by no means complete—it only illustrates some of the names that other pet owners have used.

How About . . .

ANASTASIA   EINSTEIN

BRUTUS   OBAMA

CLEOPATRA   SOCRATES

DA VINCI   WASHINGTON

Historical Names

FAMOUS POLITICAL FIGURES

Alexander

(1) The name of three of the Russian czars. (2) Alexander of Macedonia, conqueror of the ancient world, who was known as "Alexander the Great."

Blair (Tony)

Former British Prime Minister.

Bush (George W.)

The forty-third President of the United States.

Caesar (Julius)

The Roman general and statesman who became dictator of Rome, ending the era of the Roman Republic.

Castro (Fidel)

Former dictator of Cuba.

Catherine the Great

Russian Empress who succeeded to the throne after her husband's death.

Charlemagne

The great military leader who became the first Holy Roman Emperor from A.D. 800–814.

Gandhi

The great Indian statesman (1869–1948) who freed his county from British rule

through nonviolent resistance. Gandhi is considered the father of modern India.

Gorbachev (Mikhail)

Soviet leader (b. 1931) from 1985 to 1991.

Hitler

The totalitarian ruler of Germany's Third Reich who initiated World War II and was responsible for the slaughter of millions of people.

Kennedy (Teddy)

Massachusetts Senator for 46 years and brother of President John F. Kennedy and Presidential Candidate Bobby Kennedy.

Kennedy (John F.)

35th president of the United States.

Napoleon (Bonaparte)

The French general and military genius (1769–1821) who crowned himself Emperor of France and conquered much of Europe.

Obama (Barack)

First black president of the United States.

Reagan (Ronald)

The motion picture actor and California governor who became the fortieth President of the United States.

Washington (George)

First president of the United States.

Winston (Churchill)

The Prime Minister of Great Britain from 1940 to 1945 and from 1951 to 1955, who was one of the world's greatest statesmen.

GREAT MINDS THROUGH THE TIMES:

Aristotle

One of the greatest Greek thinkers and philosophers (384–322 B.C.) whose writings have had a major influence on the world.

Einstein (Albert)

The German-American physicist (1879–1955) who published the Theory of Relativity in 1905.

Freud (Sigmund)

The famous psychoanalyst (1856–1939) whose work profoundly affected the study and practice of psychology and psychiatry.

Galileo

Italian astronomer, mathematician, and physicist (1564–1642).

Mendel (Gregor)

Augustinian monk known as the father of genetics.

Newton (Sir Isaac)

The English scientist, astronomer, and mathematician (1642–1727) who invented calculus and first established the laws of gravity.

Nobel (Alfred)

Invented dynamite and established the Nobel Prize which is awarded every year for excellence in many fields.

Pavlov (Ivan Petrovich)

The Russian physiologist who won the 1904 Nobel Prize in physiology and medicine for his research on conditioned reflexes.

Plato

A famous Greek philosopher (c.428–c.348 B.C.) who was a follower of Socrates.

Socrates

A noted Greek philosopher (470–399 B.C.) whose beliefs included justice and good moral character.

Wright (Orville and Wilbur)

Credited with flying the first airplane at Kitty Hawk, North Carolina, December 17, 1903.

FAMOUS PETS THROUGH THE AGES:

Balto

A black, long-haired malamute that in February 1925 led Gunnar Kasson's dog team through a blizzard to reach diphtheria-plagued Nome, Alaska with antitoxin serum. A statue of Balto stands in New York City's Central Park.

Bessie

A collie that belonged to President Calvin Coolidge, the thirtieth President of the United States (1923–1929).

Big Ben

The fox terrier that belonged to President Herbert Hoover, named for the famous London clock.

Blacky

President Calvin Coolidge's black cat.

Buddy

The female German shepherd who was the first Seeing Eye dog. Buddy belonged to Morris Frank, a blind man from Tennessee, and was trained in Switzerland at the kennels where Dorothy Harrison Eustis, the founder of The Seeing Eye Inc., worked. Frank told Buddy's story in his book, *First Lady of Seeing Eye*.

Charlie

One of President John F. Kennedy's dogs.

Checkers

A black-and-white cocker spaniel sent to Richard Nixon when he was running for vice president. Nixon revealed Checkers' existence when he appeared on television on September 23, 1952, to combat allegations that he had received illegal campaign funds. His speech has since been called the Checkers Speech.

Chips

A shepherd-husky-collie mix that was the first member of the army's K-9 Corps sent overseas in World War II. Chips landed in Sicily in July 1943 and aided pinned-down American troops by attacking Italian gunners. He received decorations for this act and returned home in 1945.

Fido

The yellow mongrel belonging to Abraham Lincoln's two sons, Willie and Tad. Fido stayed behind in Springfield, Illinois when the President-elect and his family moved to Washington.

Laika

The female Samoyed that was the first living creature to orbit the earth in the second Soviet Sputnik.

MORE HISTORICAL NAMES

Aesop

A Greek writer of fables; lived during the late sixth century B.C.

Agrippina

The mother of the Roman emperor NERO. He had her murdered.

Ambrose (Saint)

A bishop of Milan in the fourth century A.D. who was one of the most influential men of his time.

Anastasia

A Russian imperial princess who was believed to have survived the massacre of her family, the Romanovs.

Appleseed, Johnny

John Chapman (1774–1845). The orchards of the Midwest grew from the seed that this nurseryman was reported to have spread across the land.

Attila

King of Huns called the "Scourge of God" by peoples he conquered during the fifth century.

Aztec

The Aztecs were a group of people that originated in northwest Mexico, becoming a small nomadic tribe in the twelfth century, eventually expanding into a huge empire.

Bailey (James A.)

The British circus proprietor who merged with P. T. Barnum's traveling circus in 1881.

Barney

The Scottish Terrier belonging to President George W. Bush.

Barnum (P. T.)

Phineas Taylor Barnum (1810–1891), co-founder of "The Barnum and Bailey Greatest Show on Earth."

HEROES...	
Ambrose	Merlin
Bonham	Montgomery
Bradley	Nelson
Crockett	Patton
Custer	Rommel
Grant	Sherman,
Ike	Uncle Sam

Beau
General Omar BRADLEY'S pet poodle.

Beauregard
A Confederate general whose full name was Pierre Gustave Toutant de Beauregard.

Biden (Joe)
Vice President of the United States under President Obama.

Billy the Kid
William Bonney (1859–1881). A ruthless Wild West criminal who killed a man before reaching his teens.

Bingo
The black-and-white dog on Cracker Jack boxes.

Bismarck
Otto Eduard Leopold von Bismarck (1815–1898), a Prussian statesman who united the German states into one empire and created the Triple Alliance between Germany, Austria-Hungary, and Italy, thus preserving peace in Europe until World War I.

Blackberry
One of President Calvin Coolidge's pet dogs.

Blackie
A mixed-breed dog that belonged to the author when he was a child.

Blanco
A white collie that a little girl in Illinois gave to President Lyndon B. Johnson during his term in office.

Bluegrass
Daniel BOONE'S family cat.

Bo
President Barack Obama's pet, a Portugese Water Dog.

Bonham
A hero of the Battle of the Alamo (1836).

Bradley (Omar Nelson)
An American general who commanded troops in Europe in World War II.

Brutus
The Roman general and orator who led the plot to murder Julius Caesar in 44 B.C.

Buffalo Bill
William Cody (1846–1917), was a famous hunter and scout who starred in and operated his own Wild West show.

Bush (George)
The forty-first President of the United States.

Cicero

The statesman and orator who tried to save the dying Roman Republic.

Cleopatra

The name for the seven queens of ancient Egypt. The most famous was Cleopatra VII (69–30 B.C.), who was the subject of many literary works, including Shakespeare's *Antony and Cleopatra* and *Caesar and Cleopatra* by George Bernard Shaw.

Cloe

A dog that belonged to George Washington, first President of the United States (1789–1797).

Cochise

Chief of the central Chiricahua in Southeastern Arizona (1800–1874), the most famous Apache leader to resist intrusions by whites.

Constantine

Flavius Valerius Constantinus (A.D. 280–337); also known as Constantine the Great, the first Roman emperor to adopt Christianity.

Crockett (Davy)

Famous frontiersman who died at the Battle of the Alamo (1836).

Cuba

One of Ernest Hemingway's forty cats.

Custer (George Armstrong)

The famous American army officer who lost his life in a battle against the Indians at Little Bighorn, which has become known as Custer's Last Stand.

Dubya

Former President George W. Bush's nickname.

Durkheim (Emile)

The French sociologist and founder (1859–1917) of modern sociology as an academic discipline.

Fala

The Scottish terrier that Franklin D. Roosevelt humorously defended against unjustified attacks by his political opponents.

Ferdinand

A king of Spain who, with his wife Isabella, received Christopher Columbus at the Court in Barcelona and agreed to finance his voyage.

Freebo

One of six dogs owned by President Ronald Reagan during his presidency.

Gates (Bill)

CEO of the Microsoft corporation; multi-billionaire.

Genghis Khan

The great Mongol ruler (1167–1227) who conquered a vast empire, including China.

Geronimo

Apache Indian leader (1829–1909) who eventually became a rancher. While in St. Louis for the Louisiana Purchase Exposition, he rode in President Theodore Roosevelt's inaugural parade in 1905.

Golda Meir

The woman who became Prime Minister of Israel in 1969.

Grant (Ulysses S.)

Union general during the Civil War and the eighteenth President of the United States.

Grits

The dog belonging to President Jimmy Carter's daughter, Amy.

Handsome Dan

The white bulldog that was the original Yale bulldog mascot. The first Handsome Dan has been followed by a series of namesakes, one of which still represents Yale today.

Heidi

A Weimaraner owned by President Dwight D. Eisenhower.

Her

One of the pair of beagles that accompanied President Lyndon B. Johnson and his family to the White House. Johnson received much criticism when he lifted Her and the other beagle HIM up by the ears.

Him

The other half of President Lyndon B. Johnson's pair of beagles. (See HER)

Houdini

The famous magician (1874–1926) who could escape from any contraption devised to hold him.

Igloo

The troublesome fox terrier that traveled with Admiral Richard E. Byrd on his first trip to the Antarctic (1928–1930).

Ike

The nickname of Dwight David Eisenhower, the Supreme Commander of the Allied armies in Europe in World War

II. Eisenhower later became President of the United States (1953–1961).

Isabella

Queen of Spain and wife of FERDINAND at the end of the fifteenth century.

Ivan

The name of several Russian rulers. Ivan IV (1533–1584), known as "Ivan the Terrible," was the first Russian czar.

Jackson (Stonewall)

The Confederate general during the Civil War, second only to General Robert E. Lee.

James (Jesse)

The notorious bank and train robber who vandalized the American West during the nineteenth century.

Jo-Fi

Psychoanalyst Sigmund Freud's beloved chow.

King Timahoe

The Irish setter owned by President Richard Nixon.

King Tut

One of the most famous Egyptian mummy finds. Also, President Herbert Hoover's pet German shepherd dog.

Kublai Khan

Mongol emperor (c. 1216–1294), who was the grandson of Genghis Khan.

Laddie Boy

The Airedale that belonged to President Warren G. Harding.

Lady

One of George WASHINGTON'S pet dogs.

Lee (Robert E.)

Famous general of the Confederacy during the Civil War.

Lewinsky (Monica)

Former White House intern involved in sex scandal with former President Clinton.

Liberty

President Gerald Ford's golden retriever.

Livingstone (David)

A famous British explorer who pioneered large parts of Africa during the nineteenth century.

Lucky

A black sheepdog owned by President Ronald Reagan. Of the six of President Reagan's dogs, only two resided at the White House—Lucky and REX.

Historical Names

Magellan (Ferdinand)

The Portuguese navigator who was the first person to sail around the world.

Major

A German shepherd that belonged to Franklin Delano Roosevelt.

Mao Tse-tung (Zedong)

One of the founders of the Chinese Communist Party in 1921 and the People's Republic of China in 1949.

Marco

A Pomeranian that belonged to Queen Victoria of England.

Marco Polo

A Venetian who was one of the first Europeans to travel in Asia during the late thirteenth century.

Marjorie

A diabetic black-and-white mongrel that was the first creature to be kept alive by insulin.

Maximilian

The Austrian whom the French installed as emperor of the short-lived Mexican throne (1864–1867).

Meggy

One of Franklin D. Roosevelt's pet dogs. FALA was Meggy's sire.

Merlin

The wizard and counselor of King Arthur from The *Tales of King Arthur and His Court.*

"Merlin"

Micetto

Pope Leo XII's large black-striped cat. After the Pope's death, the cat went to live with the French ambassador to Rome, the Vicomte de Chateaubriand.

Millie

(1) A mixed breed dog (part Irish setter, part collie) owned by President Ronald Reagan. (2) The English springer spaniel belonging to President and Mrs. George Bush. Mrs. Bush wrote a book about Millie.

Ming

The dynasty that ruled China from 1368 to 1644. The Ming period was one of artistic growth.

Montgomery (Bernard Law)

The British general who won fame during the African campaign and the invasion of Europe in World War II.

Mopsey

One of George WASHINGTON'S favorite dogs.

Moshe Dayan

A leading Israeli general and statesman (1915–1981).

Mushka

A dog that was placed in orbit by the Russians in one of the first Sputnik space vehicles.

Neff (Pat)

A governor of Texas during the first half of the twentieth century and a president of Baylor University in Waco, Texas.

Nelson

A black cat, the favorite of Sir Winston Churchill, Prime Minister of Great Britain during most of World War II.

Nelson (Horatio)

Great Britain's greatest admiral and naval hero, who established Britain's rule of the seas in the 1800s.

Nero

One of the cruelest Roman emperors, who killed thousands of Christians.

Niña, Pinta, and Santa Maria

The three ships in Christopher Columbus's fleet when he discovered America on October 12, 1492.

Nipper

The fox terrier that appears with a phonograph in the RCA trademark.

Nobel (Alfred)

Invented dynamite and established the Nobel Prize which is awarded every year for excellence in many fields.

Historical Names

Obama (Michelle)

First lady and wife of President Barack Obama.

Patton (George Smith)

An American general (1885–1945) who led the 3rd Army in Europe during World War II.

Perruque

One of fourteen cats owned by Cardinal Richelieu when he died in 1642.

Pompey the Great

Roman general and statesman (106–48 B.C.) who was one of Julius Caesar's greatest adversaries.

Pompidou (Georges)

Premier and President (1911–1974) of France's Fifth Republic from 1962–1974.

Powell (Colin)

Secretary of State under the Bush Administration.

Princess Diana

Born Diana Spencer in 1961, she married Prince Charles in 1981. She lived a high-profile life until her tragic and untimely death in 1997.

Pushinka

A puppy from STRELKA'S litter that the Soviet Premier Nikita Khrushchev presented to Mrs. John F. Kennedy when she was First Lady.

Rasputin

The religious man (1865–1916) who corrupted Russia's Czar Nicholas II and his wife Alexandra. Many attribute Rasputin to the Romanov's downfall.

Rex

A spaniel that belonged to President Ronald Reagan.

Ripley (Robert Leroy)

An American cartoonist who began collecting strange and unusual facts that he eventually compiled into two *Believe It or Not* books.

Rob Roy

President Calvin Coolidge's white collie.

Rommel (Erwin)

The brilliant German general (1891–1994) who commanded the Afrika Korps and the forces defending Normandy in World War II.

Ross (Betsy)

Creator of the first U.S. flag.

Rover

The collie that was President Lyndon Johnson's first dog.

Rufus

A poodle owned by British Prime Minister Winston Churchill.

Sailor Boy

Theodore Roosevelt's pet dog.

Scannon

Meriwether Lewis's black Newfoundland that accompanied the Lewis and Clark expedition to the Pacific.

Searcher

One of George WASHINGTON's pet dogs.

Shannon

A dog that was the White House pet of John F. Kennedy, Jr.

Sharon (Ariel)

Prime Minister of Israel.

Shasta

The first U.S.-born *liger,* the offspring of a male lion and a female tiger, to reach maturity. Shasta was born May 6, 1948, at the Hogle Zoological Garden in Salt Lake City, Utah.

Sherman (William Tecumseh)

The famous Union general during the American Civil War.

Sizi

The cat that was a companion to Albert Schweitzer (1875–1965) when he was a medical missionary in Africa.

Skip

A mongrel dog owned by President Theodore Roosevelt.

Socks

A cat that belonged to former President Clinton.

Stanley (Henry)

The British explorer who led the expedition to find David LIVINGSTONE.

Strelka

One of the two female Samoyeds that the Soviet Union launched in Sputnik V on August 19, 1960.

Taca

A Siberian husky owned by President Ronald Reagan.

Thatcher (Margaret)

The former Prime Minister of Great Britain who was known as the "Iron Lady."

Thurmond (Strom)

Died at 100 years of age, the lomgest-serving member of the U.S. Senate (South Carolina, Republican).

Tito

The Communist ruler of Yugoslavia after World War II. Tito declared Yugoslavia's independence from Soviet control.

Trafalgar

The cape on Spain's southern coast at the western entrance to the Strait of Gibraltar that was the sight of one of history's greatest naval battles: Great Britain, led by Admiral Horatio Nelson, defeated the combined French and Spanish fleets on October 21, 1805.

CONQUERORS AND VILLIANS...	
Attila	Ivan
Billy the Kid	Jesse James
Brutus	Kublai Khan
Genghis Khan	Rasputin

Traveler

The horse of Robert E. Lee, the Confederate general during the American Civil War.

Trojan

An inhabitant of Troy, an ancient city in Asia Minor that Homer made famous.

Uncle Sam

The personification of the United States; his top hat and red, white, and blue clothes make him a distinctive figure.

Victory

A golden retriever owned by President Ronald Reagan.

Viking

A member of the Scandinavian bands of sea rovers who raided England, Ireland, France, Germany, Italy, and Spain between the 700s and 1100s. The Vikings also settled Greenland and Iceland.

Voltaire

Eighteenth-century French man of letters; defended those unjustly persecuted by the Church.

Watson

(1) Alexander Graham Bell's assistant. (2) Sherlock Holmes's friend and assistant in the Arthur Conan Doyle fictional mysteries.

Winston (Churchill)

The Prime Minister of Great Britain from 1940 to 1945 and from 1951 to 1955, who was one of the world's greatest statesmen.

Yeltsin (Boris)

Former Russian President and Nobel Prize winner.

Yuki

The small white dog adopted by President Lyndon B. Johnson in November 1966. Yuki quickly became the President's favorite dog.

Zedillo (Ernesto)

Former Mexican President.

"Winston"

ATHENA

6

Greek and Roman Mythology

The gods, goddesses, and other figures of mythology are known for both their colorful appearance and their vibrant personalities; furthermore, they generally have unusual, and therefore, memorable names. Thus, pets often are namesakes of these characters, and a pet's mythological name can provide a great source of conversation.

How About . . .

Achilles	Hades
Aphrodite	Hector
Apollo	Hercules
Ares	Zeus
Artemis	

MYTHICAL HEROES

Achilles

The champion of the Greeks in the Trojan War.

Aeneas

The son of APHRODITE (Venus) who fought for TROY in the Trojan War. After the defeat he escaped to Italy where he founded the Roman race.

Hector

The brave, noble son of King PRIAM of TROY. Hector was the Trojan champion in the Trojan War.

Hercules

The Roman name for HERACLES, Greece's greatest hero and the strongest man alive. Son of Zeus.

Jason

The leader of the quest for the GOLDEN FLEECE.

Odysseus

The Greek hero of the Trojan War, known for his cunning. Main character in Homer's *The Odyssey*.

Perseus

The hero who killed MEDUSA and was the faithful husband of ANDROMEDA.

Remus

One of the twin brothers who founded Rome. As children, they were washed ashore by the Tiber and saved by a she-wolf who fed them her milk. (See ROMULUS.)

Romulus

REMUS'S twin brother who helped found Rome. (See REMUS.)

Theseus

The greatest Athenian hero.

Ulysses

Another name for ODYSSEUS.

POWERFUL MONSTERS AND VILLAINS

Circe

A beautiful and dangerous witch who turned men into beasts.

Cottus

A monster with a hundred hands.

Gorgon

Dragonlike creatures with wings and snakes for hair, whose look turned men to stone.

Hydra

A nine-headed creature killed by HERACLES. (See HERCULES.)

Ixion

The first murderer. Ixion also attempted to seduce HERA. ZEUS sentenced him to eternal punishment in HADES, where he was tied to a wheel and lashed with serpents.

Larvae

The spirits of HADES'S wicked dead, who were greatly feared.

Lycus

Ruler of THEBES and the husband of DIRCE. His daughter killed him because of his cruelty.

Medusa

One of the GORGONS. PERSEUS cut off her head.

Nemean Lion, The

The ferocious lion that ravaged the valley of Nemea, until Heracles (HERCULES) strangled the beast to death.

Procrustes

A man who tied his victims onto an iron bed and cut or stretched them to fit on the bed. THESEUS killed Procrustes in the same manner.

Siren

One of the creatures with beautiful voices who lived on an island in the sea and lured sailors to their deaths.

Sphinx

The creature shaped like a winged lion with the breast and face of a woman. She besieged THEBES until OEDIPUS answered her riddle.

Thespian Lion, The

A lion that ravaged livestock around Mount Cithaeron until Heracles (HERCULES) killed it.

Typhoeus

Another name for TYPHON.

Typhon

The monster with a hundred heads whom ZEUS conquered.

THE OLYMPIAN GODS

Aphrodite

The Goddess of Love and Beauty.

Apollo

The God of Light and Truth.

Ares

The God of War (Roman: Mars). The Son of ZEUS and HERA; he was a bully and also a coward, detested by his parents as well as others.

Artemis

The Goddess of Hunting and Wild Things.

Athena

The Goddess of the City, Protector of Civilized Life, Handicrafts, and Agriculture.

Demeter

The Goddess of Corn. Sister of ZEUS, she bore him a daughter, PERSEPHONE.

Dionysus

The God of Wine.

Hades

The God of the Underworld. He was the son of CRONUS and RHEA. (Hades is also used as a name for the Underworld itself.)

Hephaestus

The God of Fire.

Hera

ZEUS'S wife and sister. She was the Protector of Marriage and Married Women.

Hermes

ZEUS'S messenger. He was sometimes called the "Master Thief."

Hestia

The Goddess of the Hearth.

Poseidon

The God of the Sea, who was CRONUS'S son and ZEUS'S brother.

Zeus

The Supreme God of the Universe.

LEGENDARY PETS

Argos

ODYSSEUS'S dog. After being away at the Trojan War for twenty years, Odysseus returned to his home disguised as a beggar, and only Argos recognized him. The dog, too sick and weak to walk, wagged his tail in recognition; however, afraid of revealing his identity, Odysseus didn't acknowledge Argos, and as Odysseus walked on, Argos died.

Arion

The first horse, an offspring of POSEIDON.

Cerberus

The huge, fearsome watchdog of HADES. Cerberus guarded the gates of Hades, preventing spirits from leaving.

Maera

A faithful dog, whose master ICARIUS was murdered and thrown into a well. Maera led Icarius's daughter ERIGONE to the body. She hanged herself and the dog then jumped into the well.

Pegasus

The winged horse that sprang from MEDUSA'S blood when PERSEUS killed her.

MORE GREEK AND ROMAN MYTHOLOGY

Achelous

A River God who turned himself into a bull to fight Heracles (see HERCULES) because the two men were both in love with the same woman, Deianira.

Actaeon

A young hunter whom ARTEMIS turned into a stag because he had accidentally seen her naked. In his new form, Actaeon's own dogs chased and killed him.

Adonis

APHRODITE'S love, who spent half the year with her and the other half in the Underworld. A boar killed him, and a crimson flower sprung up where each drop of his blood fell.

Aero

ORION'S love and the daughter of the King of Chios.

Aidos

The personified emotion of reverence and shame, which was esteemed highest of all feelings.

Ajax

One of the Greek champions in the Trojan War.

Alce

One of ACTAEON'S hounds; the name means "strength."

Alexander

Another name for PARIS, who caused the Trojan War and died of a wound from a poisoned arrow.

Althea

The mother of Meleager; she killed him and then killed herself.

Amazon

A member of the nation of women warriors who had no dealings with men except to oppose them in war and to breed children.

Andromeda

The daughter of CASSIOPEIA, who was punished for her mother's vanity. PERSEUS saved her from her fate, and she married him.

Antigone

The daughter of OEDIPUS. She was killed by CREON, his successor on the throne.

Arcas

The son of CALLISTO and ZEUS whom Zeus placed among the stars as Ursa Minor (Lesser Bear).

Argus

HERA'S watchman with a hundred eyes.

Ariadne

King MINOS'S daughter who was deserted on the island of NAXOS by her lover, THESEUS.

Arne

Regarded as the ancestress of the Boeotian Greeks.

Asbolos

One of ACTAEON'S hounds; the name means "soot-color."

Asopus

A River God.

Atalanta

The maiden who could outshoot, outrun, and outwrestle most men. She eventually was turned into a lioness.

Ate

The Goddess of Mischief. Although a daughter of ZEUS, she was cast out of OLYMPUS.

Atlas

The TITAN who held the world on his shoulders.

Attica

The country around Athens.

Aurora

The Goddess of Dawn.

Bacchus

Roman name for DIONYSUS, the God of the Vine.

Banos

One of ACTAEON'S hounds.

Battus

A peasant who saw HERMES steal APOLLO'S cattle. Hermes turned Battus into stone because the man broke his promise not to reveal the identity of the thief to Apollo.

"Ate"

Baucis

A poor old woman who was blessed by the gods, given a temple to live in, and promised that she would never live alone without her husband.

Bellona

The Roman name for ENYO, the Goddess of War.

Belus

The grandfather of the Danaïds (who were condemned to carry water in jars that were forever leaking).

Biton

One of the two sons of Cydippe, a priestess of HERA. He and his brother yoked themselves to a wagon to carry their mother to pray. The journey killed both sons.

Boötes

The constellation just behind the Dipper. See ICARIUS.

Boreas

(1) The God of the North Wind who kidnapped and ravished Orithyia. (2) One of ACTAEON'S hounds.

Bromius

Another name for DIONYSUS, who was a son of ZEUS. (See BACCHUS.)

Brontes

One of three CYCLOPS, each of whom had only one eye in the middle of his forehead.

Cabeiri

Dwarfs with supernatural powers. They protected the fields of Lemnos.

Cacus

The giant who stole cattle from Heracles' (HERCULES') flock.

Calliope

The daughter of ZEUS who was the MUSE of Epic Poetry.

Callisto

LYCAON'S daughter who was seduced by ZEUS and bore him a son, ARCAS. In a jealous rage, HERA turned Callisto into a bear, and when Arcas grew up placed his mother before him so that he would kill her. Zeus, however, saved Callisto and put her up in the stars as Ursa Major (Great Bear), placing Arcas beside her as Ursa Minor (Lesser Bear).

Calpe

The ancient Greek name for the Rock of Gibraltar.

Calypso

A nymph who kept ODYSSEUS prisoner on her island.

Camilla

A very skilled maiden warrior who was followed by a band of warriors.

Canache

One of ACTAEON'S hounds; the name means "ringwood."

Cassandra

One of PRIAM'S daughters. She became a prophetess because APOLLO loved her and gave her power of prognostication. Unfortunately, her prophecies were never believed.

Castor

The brother of POLLUX and the son of LEDA. He and his brother were the Protectors of Sailors.

Centaur

A creature who was half man and half horse.

Ceres

The Roman name for DEMETER.

Chaos

The Nothingness that existed before the gods and before Creation.

Charites

Another name for the Graces who attended APHRODITE.

Charon

The boatman who guided the ferry that carried the dead souls to the gates of HADES.

Chediatros

One of ACTAEON'S hounds.

Cisseta

One of ACTAEON'S hounds.

Cleobis

BITON'S brother, son of Cydippe, a priestess of HERA. Cleobis perished with his brother after they yoked themselves to a wagon carrying their mother to pray.

Clio

The MUSE of History.

Clytie

A maiden who loved the Sun God, but whose love was not returned. She stared at him with longing until she turned into a sunflower.

Cora

Another name for PERSEPHONE.

Coran

One of ACTAEON'S hounds; the name means "crop-eared."

Coronis

A maiden whom APOLLO loved, but who did not love him. She was unfaithful, so he killed her.

Creon

The brother of JOCASTA. Creon became regent after OEDIPUS resigned the throne.

Cronus

A titan who was the father of ZEUS.

Cupid

Latin for EROS, the Greek God of Love.

Cyclops

A giant with only one eye in the middle of his forehead.

Cyllo

One of ACTAEON'S hounds; the name means "halt."

Cyllopotes

One of ACTAEON'S hounds; the name means "zigzagger."

Cynthia

Another name for ARTEMIS.

Cyprian

Another name for APHRODITE.

Cyprios

One of ACTAEON'S hounds.

ACTAEON'S HOUNDS . . .	
Alce	Echnobas
Asbolos	Eudromos
Banos	Harpale
Cisseta	Ichnobate
Cyllopotes	Lelaps
Cyprios	Melanea
Draco	Pterelas
Dromas	

Cyprus

The island where APHRODITE was born.

Dactyls

The women of Mount Ida, who were the first to make implements of iron.

Daphne

A huntress whose father, the River God Peneus, changed her into a tree to protect her from APOLLO who loved her.

Delian

Another name for APOLLO.

Delos

The island where APOLLO was born and where his temple stood.

Delphi

The site of APOLLO'S oracles.

Diana

The Roman name for ARTEMIS.

Dido

The founder and queen of Carthage. She threw herself on a pyre when AENEAS, whom she loved, left to search for a homeland in Italy.

Diomedes

A great Greek warrior at TROY.

Dione

A minor goddess. By some accounts, Dione and Zeus were APHRODITE'S parents.

Dirce

The wife of LYCUS, the ruler of THEBES. Her grandsons and daughter killed her by tying her hair to a bull.

Dodona

ZEUS'S oracle, the oldest in Greece.

Dorian

A member of one of the principal groups of ancient Greeks.

Doris

One of the 3,000 daughters of Ocean and wife NEREUS.

Draco

One of ACTAEON'S hounds; the name means "the dragon."

Dromas

One of ACTAEON'S hounds; the name means "the courser."

Dromios

One of ACTAEON'S hounds; the name means "seize 'em."

Dryad

One of the nymphs of the trees.

Echnobas

One of ACTAEON'S hounds.

Echo

The fairest of the nymphs who loved NARCISSUS; HERA condemned her never to talk unless she repeated what someone else had already said.

Electra

The daughter of Agamemnon and Clytemnestra. She avenged her father's murder by inciting her brother, ORESTES, to kill their mother and her lover.

Enyo

The Goddess of War.

Erato

The MUSE of Love Poetry.

Erigone

The daughter of ICARIUS, who hanged herself after finding her father murdered. DIONYSUS placed her in the heavens as Virgo.

Eris

The sister of ARES whose name means "discord."

Eros

The God of Love.

Eudromos

One of ACTAEON'S hounds; the name means "good runner."

Europa

A maiden with whom ZEUS fell in love. As a bull, he carried her off to Crete. The continent of Europe was named for her.

Eurus

The God of the East Wind.

Fauna

The Roman Goddess of Fertility, sometimes called the Good Goddess.

Favonius

The Latin name for the West Wind.

Flora

The Roman Flower Goddess.

Galatea

(1) A sea nymph whom Polyphemus, the cyclops, loved. (2) The name of PYGMALION'S statue, which came to life.

Gemini

The constellation of the twin brothers, CASTOR and POLLUX.

Harmonia

Cadmus's wife, who was the daughter of ARES and APHRODITE.

Harpale

One of ACTAEON'S hounds; the name means "voracious."

Hebe

The Goddess of Youth. She was the daughter of ZEUS and HERA.

Hecate

A triple deity who was Goddess of the Moon, Goddess of the Earth, and Goddess of the Underworld.

Hecuba

The queen of TROY and wife of King PRIAM.

Helen

The daughter of ZEUS and LEDA, who was the fairest woman in the world. She married MENELAUS, but PARIS kidnapped her, starting the Trojan War.

Helicon

One of the MUSES' mountains. It was sacred to APOLLO whose temple was there.

Helios

The Sun God.

Heracles

See HERCULES.

Hermione

Unaware she had been promised to Orestes, MENELAUS gave her to ACHILLES' son, Pyrrhus.

Hero

The ill-fated lover of LEANDER. He died, and she killed herself.

Herse

An Athenian princess who was beloved by Hermes.

Hesper

The Goddess of the Evening Star.

Hesperides

The daughter of ATLAS, who with LADON (2), guarded the trees with golden branches, golden leaves, and golden apples.

Hilara

The daughter of APOLLO. Her name means "laughter-loving."

Himeros

The God of Desire who attended EROS. Also called Longing.

Hippodamia

Wife of PELOPS. He won her in a chariot race.

Hippolytus

The son of THESEUS whose second wife, PHAEDRA, fell in love with Hippolytus.

Hyacinth

A companion of APOLLO. He was accidentally killed when Apollo's discus hit him in the head. On each spot where a drop of his blood fell, a Hyacinth flower arose.

Hyades

Some nymphs whom ZEUS placed as the stars that bring rain when they are near the horizon.

Hypnos

The God of Sleep.

Iacchus

Another name for DIONYSUS. (See BACCHUS.)

Ibycus

A poet who lived around 550 B.C. When robbers left him mortally wounded he asked the cranes that were flying overhead to avenge him, and they did.

Icarius

An Athenian, in Greek mythology, whom DIONYSUS taught how to make wine. Drunken shepherds murdered Icarius and threw him down a well, where his faithful dog, MAERA, found him. Dionysus honored Icarius, placing him among the stars as the constellation BOÖTES.

Icarus

The son of Daedalus, the architect. When Icarus flew too near the sun, the wax that held his wings in place melted. Icarus fell to earth and was killed.

Icelus

The son of HYPNOS, who had the power to change himself into all sorts of birds and animals.

Ichnobate

One of ACTAEON'S hounds; the name means "tracker."

Ida

A nymph who took care of ZEUS when he was being hidden from Cronus.

Inachus

The father of IO.

Ino

The Sea Goddess who saved ODYSSEUS from drowning.

Io

The maiden who had an affair with ZEUS. He turned her into a white heifer to protect her from HERA'S jealous wrath. Unfortunately, Io, wound up in Hera's possession and spent years trying to escape and return to her original form. Finally, Zeus restored Io's humanity, and she spent the rest of her days happily.

Iphicles

Heracles' (HERCULES) half brother.

Iris

The Goddess of the Rainbow.

Janus

A NUMINA who became personified. Janus was the God of Good Beginnings.

Jocasta

OEDIPUS'S mother and wife.

Jove

Another name for ZEUS.

Juna

The Roman name for HERA.

Jupiter

The Roman name for ZEUS.

Juturna

The Roman Goddess of Springs.

Kora

Another name for PERSEPHONE.

Labros

One of ACTAEON'S hounds; the name means "furious."

Lacena

One of ACTAEON'S hounds; the name means "lioness."

Lachne

One of ACTAEON'S hounds; the name means "glossy."

Lacon

One of ACTAEON'S hounds.

Ladon

(1) One of ACTAEON'S hounds. (2) The serpent who guarded the Golden Apples of the HESPERIDES.

Laertes

ODYSSEUS'S father.

Laius

The father of OEDIPUS. Oedipus unwittingly murdered him.

Lampos

One of ACTAEON'S hounds; the name means "shining one."

Lar

A NUMINA, who was the spirit of an ancestor. Every Roman family had a Lar.

Latinus

The great-grandson of SATURN and the king of the city of LATIUM.

Latium

A city in Italy that was conquered by AENEAS.

Latona

Another name for LETO.

Lavinia

The daughter of LATINUS and the wife of AENEAS. Together, husband and wife founded the Roman race.

Leander

HERO'S lover who killed herself after he drowned swimming to a rendezvous with her.

Leda

The wife of King Tyndareus of Sparta. ZEUS, in the form of a swan, seduced her.

Lelaps

(1) One of ACTAEON'S hounds; the name means "hurricane." (2) The hound destined to chase a fox until ZEUS finally changed them both to stone.

Lemures

Another name for LARVAE.

Lethe

The River of Forgetfulness in the Underworld.

Leto

Daughter of TITANS; APOLLO and ARTEMIS were her children by ZEUS.

Leucos

One of ACTAEON'S hounds; the name means "gray."

Liber

Another name for BACCHUS.

Libera

A Roman name for PERSEPHONE. She was abducted by PLUTO, who wanted her to be queen of the Underworld.

Libitina

The Roman Goddess of the Dead.

Linus

The son of APOLLO and Psamathe. When his mother deserted him, dogs tore him apart.

Lotis

A nymph who was changed into a lotus tree.

Lucina

Sometimes regarded as the Roman Goddess of Childbirth.

Luna

Latin for the Goddess of the Moon. The name Luna referred to DIANA.

Lyaeus

Another name for BACCHUS.

Lycaon

A king of ATTICA and the father of CALLISTO. When he served human flesh at a banquet, ZEUS turned him into a wolf.

Lycisca

One of ACTAEON'S hounds.

Lyncea

One of ACTAEON'S hounds.

Machaon

The Greeks' physician during the Trojan War.

Machimos

One of ACTAEON'S hounds; the name means "boxer."

Maeander

River in Phrygia that frequently changes its course.

Maia

VULCAN'S wife. (See HEPHATETUS.)

Manes

The spirits of the good dead in HADES.

Mars

Roman name for ARES.

Medea

The daughter of King Colchias. A sorceress, she fell in love with JASON and helped him on his quest for the GOLDEN FLEECE.

Megara

The wife of Heracles (HERCULES) and mother of three of his sons. Hercules went mad and killed them all.

Melampus

A great soothsayer whose pet snakes taught him animal language.

Melanchete

One of ACTAEON'S hounds; the name means "black-coated."

Melanea

One of ACTAEON'S hounds; the name means "black."

Melanion

The runner who beat ATALANTA and won her love.

Melpomene

The MUSE of Tragedy.

Menelaus

The brother of Agamemnon and husband of HELEN.

Menelea

One of ACTAEON'S hounds.

Mentor

ODYSSEUS'S most trusted friend. ATHENA disguised herself as Mentor when she appeared to TELEMACHUS.

Mercury

The Roman name for HERMES.

Metis

ZEUS'S first wife, also called Prudence. Zeus swallowed her and developed a monumental headache, which eased only after ATHENA sprang from his head.

Midas

A king of Phrygia whose wish that everything he touched would turn to gold was granted.

Minerva

The Roman name for ATHENA.

Minos

One of the three judges in the Underworld.

Minotaur

A monster that was half bull and half human.

Minyas

The king of THESSALY. The ARGONAUTS, sometimes called the Minyae, were his descendants.

Moira

Fate, a mysterious power stronger than the gods. One who scorned Moira would meet NEMESIS.

Molossos

One of ACTAEON'S hounds.

Moly

An herb with white blossoms that HERMES gave ODYSSEUS to protect him from CIRCE'S spells.

Mopsus

Soothsayer of the ARGONAUTS, he also went on the Calydonian boar hunt.

Morpheus

The God of Sleep; also called the God of Dreams.

Mors

The God of Death; also called Thanatos.

Muse

Nine daughters of ZEUS and Mnemosyne. They were goddesses of memory and then of the arts and sciences.

THE MUSES . . .	
Calliope	Polyhymnia
Clio	Terpsichore
Erato	Thalia
Euterpe	Urania
Melpomene	

Myrmidon

One of a group of soldiers who fought against the TROJANS.

Napa

One of ACTAEON'S hounds; the name means "sired by a wolf."

Narcissus

A beautiful boy who scorned love despite many admiring ladies. Finally, he was cursed, fell in love with himself, and pined away for his own reflection in a pond.

Naxos

The island where THESEUS left ARIADNE.

Neleus

One of the twin sons of TYRO and POSEIDON.

Nemesis

The Goddess of Righteous Anger, the personified emotion esteemed highest of all feelings.

Neptune

The Roman name for POSEIDON.

Nereid

A nymph of the sea and the daughter of NEREUS.

Nereus

The Old Man of the Sea. He had the power of prophecy and could assume any form he desired.

Nessus

A centaur who gave Heracles' (HERCULES') wife, Deianira, his blood as a love potion when he was dying.

Nestor

The wisest and oldest of the Greek chieftans.

Nike

The Greek Goddess of Victory.

Notus

The God of the South Wind.

Numina

The powers that were the Roman gods before the Romans adopted the Greek ones.

Ocydroma

One of ACTAEON'S hounds; the name means "swift runner."

Ocyrrhoe

A prophetess.

Oedipus

The king who was fated to kill his father and marry his mother.

Olympus

A mountain peak in Greece and home of the gods.

Ophion

A great serpent that ruled the TITANS before CRONUS.

Ops

The wife of SATURN (see CRONUS), who was the Goddess of the Harvest.

Orcus

The Roman name for the King of the Dead. (See HADES, PLUTO.)

Orestes

The son of Agamemnon and Clytemnestra. He avenged his father's murder by killing his mother and her lover.

Oribasos

One of ACTAEON'S hounds; the name means "mountain-ranger."

Orion

ARTEMIS'S hunter. After she killed him, he was placed in the sky as a constellation.

Orpheus

The greatest mortal musician. He journeyed to the Underworld to find his dead bride, EURYDICE.

Orthia

Another name for ARTEMIS.

Ossa

A mountain in THESSALY once inhabited by centaurs.

Otus

One of twin brothers, both giants, who wanted to prove themselves superior to the gods. ARTEMIS killed them for their presumption by making them accidentally kill each other.

Paean

The physician to the gods; also, APOLLO as healer.

Pales

The Strengthener of Cattle.

Palladium

The sacred image of ATHENA in TROY that protected the city as long as it was kept there.

Pamphagos

One of ACTAEON'S hounds; the name means "ravenous."

Pan

The God of the Goatherds and Shepherds who was part goat and part man.

Pandora

The first woman created by ZEUS; she brought evil into the world.

Panope

One of the sea nymphs.

Paphos

The daughter of the lovers PYGMALION and GALATEA, who gave her name to APHRODITE'S favorite city.

Paris

The TROJAN who kidnapped HELEN, starting the Trojan War.

Parthenon

ATHENA'S temple in Athens.

Peitho

The Goddess of Persuasion. She was the daughter of HERMES and APHRODITE.

Pelasgus

The ancestor of the Pelasgian—one of the earliest groups to inhabit the islands and mainland of Greece and Anaholia.

Peleus

ACHILLES' father. He was one of the ARGONAUTS.

Pelias

One of the twin sons of TYRO and POSEIDON.

Pelops

The son of TANTALUS. He was killed by his father, boiled in a cauldron, and served to the gods to eat.

Penates

The Gods of the Hearth and the Guardians of the Storehouse.

Penelope

ODYSSEUS'S faithful wife.

Pentheus

King of THEBES who was killed by the Bacchae when he was caught watching their secret rites.

Pergamos

The holy place of TROY.

Persephone

The Queen of the Underworld and wife of HADES.

Phaedra

ARIADNE'S sister and wife of THESEUS. When she fell in love with his son, HIPPOLYTUS, she killed herself.

Phaëthon

The son of APOLLO, whose wish to drive his father's chariot for one day almost led to the end of the world.

Phantasus
Variously, the son or brother of HYPNOS. Phantasus was the God of Dreams of Inanimate Objects.

Phaon
An old boatman to whom APHRODITE gave youth and beauty for ferrying her from Lesbos to Chios.

Philemon
A poor old man who with his wife was blessed by the gods, given a temple to live in, and promised that he would never live alone without her.

Phineus
A prophet whom ZEUS cursed by having HARPIES defile his food whenever he wanted to eat.

Phobos
The God of Fear. He accompanied ARES into battle.

Phoebe
A TITAN who was the first Moon Goddess.

Pholus
A centaur-friend of Heracles (HERCULES).

Pirene
Famous spring in Corinth.

Pittheus
King of Troezen and the father of THESEUS'S mother.

Pluto
The God of the Underworld. (See HADES.)

Plutus
The God of Wealth, a Roman allegorical figure.

Poena
The Roman Goddess of Punishment. The Greeks regarded her as an attendant of NEMESIS.

Pollux
The son of LEDA, who with his brother CASTOR was the Special Protector of Sailors.

Polybus
King of CORINTH, whom OEDIPUS believed was his father.

Polydeuces
Another name for POLLUX.

Polydorus
A son of PRIAM. According to Homer, he was killed by ACHILLES.

Polyidus
A wise seer of Corinth.

Polyxena

HECUBA'S daughter who was killed on ACHILLES' grave.

Pomenis

One of ACTAEON'S hounds; the name means "leader."

Pomona

The first NUMINA. She was later personified and became the Goddess of Gardens and Orchards.

Pontus

The God of the Deep Sea. He was a son of Mother Earth and the father of the Sea God NEREUS.

Priam

King of TROY, during the war against the Greeks.

Priapus

The God of Fertility.

Procne

PHILOMELA'S sister, who avenged her sister's punishment by killing her own son and feeding him to her husband, TEREUS. The gods changed her into a nightingale.

Procris

The niece of PROCNE and PHILOMELA, who was accidentally killed with her husband's javelin.

Proetus

The king of ARGOS.

Prometheus

The Titan whose name means "forethought." He sided with ZEUS in his war with the TITANS.

Proserpine

Another name for PERSEPHONE.

Proteus

The god sometimes said to be POSEIDON'S son and sometimes said to be his attendant. Proteus could foretell the future and change his shape, at will.

Psyche

A beautiful maiden who married CUPID and was given immortality.

Pterelas

One of ACTAEON'S hounds; the name means "winged."

Pygmalion

The sculptor who fell in love with his statue of a woman. APHRODITE brought the sculpture to life, as GALATEA, and the two were married.

Pylades

ORESTES' friend and cousin who helped avenge Agamemnon's murder.

Pylos

NESTOR'S home.

Pyramus

The beautiful youth who loved THISBE and killed himself because he thought she was dead. The red fruit of the mulberry is a memorial to the lovers.

Pyrrha

One of two people saved from the Flood that destroyed the world.

Python

A serpent killed by APOLLO.

Rhea

CRONUS'S sister-queen. She was the mother of ZEUS, POSEIDON, HADES, DEMETER, HERA, and HESTIA.

Rhesus

The TROJANS' Thracian ally, whose horses surpassed all mortal ones.

Salmoneus

A man who pretended to be ZEUS. The god struck him down with a lightning bolt.

Sarpedon

The son of ZEUS and EUROPA. He fought with the TROJANS against the Greeks.

Saturn

The Roman name for CRONUS.

Satyrs

Goat-men who were followers of PAN.

Scamander

The name used by mortals for the great river of TROY (called Xanthos by the gods).

Scheria

The country of the Phaeacians in the Odyssey.

Sciron

A man who made those he captured kneel to wash his feet and then would kick them down to the sea. THESEUS threw him over a precipice.

Scorpio

The scorpion, one of the signs of the Zodiac.

Scylla

A sea nymph whom CIRCE changed into a monster with serpents and dogs' heads coming from her body. Scylla destroyed all sailors who passed her.

Scyros

The island where THESEUS died and ACHILLES disguised himself as a girl.

Selene

The Moon Goddess. Selene was one of ARTEMIS'S three forms.

Selli

The people who made bread from acorns in ZEUS'S sacred grove.

Semele

DIONYSUS'S mother whom ZEUS loved.

Sibyl

A prophetess who guided AENEAS to the Underworld.

Sidero

TYRO'S maid who married her husband and was killed by Tyro's son, PELIAS.

Sileni

Followers of DIONYSUS and PAN, who were part man and part horse.

Silenus

A jovial fat old man who was always drunk. He was said to be PAN'S brother or son.

Simois

One of the rivers of TROY.

Sirius

The Dog Star in the constellation Canis Major.

Sol

The Roman God of the sun.

Sterope

One of ATLAS'S daughters who was placed in the heavens as a star.

Stricta

One of ACTAEON'S hounds; the name means "spot."

Styx

The river of the unbreakable oath in the Underworld. Anyone who broke such an oath was banished from the council of the gods and denied nectar and ambrosia.

Sylvanus

One of the NUMINA; the Helper of Plowmen and Woodcutters.

Syracuse

The greatest city of Sicily.

Syrinx

A nymph loved by PAN. Her sister nymphs turned her into a tuft of reeds to save her from him, but he made the reeds into a pipe.

Talus

Last of the Bronze race. Talus was made completely of bronze except for one ankle.

Tantalus

ZEUS'S son whom the gods loved. Tantalus hated the gods and served them his son to eat. They discovered his treachery and punished him by putting him in HADES in a pool that drained whenever he tried to drink. They also placed fruit trees above him from which he could never pick fruit.

Tartarus
Another name for the Underworld.

Telamon
The father of AJAX. He was one of the ARGONAUTS.

Telemachus
The son of ODYSSEUS.

Telephus
Heracles' (HERCULES') son. He fought with the Greeks against the TROJANS.

Tempe
A beautiful valley near Mount Olympus.

Tereus
PROCNE'S husband. He was changed into a hawk.

Terminus
A NUMINA who was the Guardian of Boundaries.

Thalia
The MUSE of Comedy. She was also one of the three Graces.

Thamyris
A poet who was struck blind when he challenged the MUSES to a contest.

Thea
A TITAN who married her brother Hyperion and gave birth to the sun.

Thebes
The city founded by Cadmus.

Themis
Right or Divine Justice which sat beside ZEUS in OLYMPUS.

Theridamas
One of ACTAEON'S hounds; the name means "beast-tamer."

Theron
One of ACTAEON'S hounds; the name means "savage-faced."

Thessaly
The site of Mount OLYMPUS in northeastern Greece.

Thestius
A king of Calydon who was the father of LEDA and ALTHEA.

Thetis
The sea nymph who was the mother of ACHILLES.

Thisbe

PYRAMUS'S lover who killed herself after she found him dead. The red fruit of the mulberry tree is a memorial to them.

LESSER GODS . . .	
Asopus	Hesper
Ate	Hestia
Aurora	Hypnos
Demeter	Ino
Dione	Iris
Enyo	Morpheus
Eros	Mors
Eurus	Nemesis
Fauna	Peitho
Hebe	Phobos
Hecate	Selene
Helios	Tyche
Hephaestus	

Thoös

One of ACTAEON'S hounds; the name means "swift."

Thrace

The home of a fierce people in the northeast of Greece.

Tiber

The God of the Tiber River, who instructed AENEAS to go to the site of Rome.

Titan

The elder gods who were huge and strong and ruled over the universe before ZEUS dethroned them.

Tityus

A giant killed by APOLLO and ARTEMIS.

Triton

The Trumpeter of the Sea. He was a son of POSEIDON.

Trivia

Another name for HECATE.

Trojan

An inhabitant of the city of TROY. (See also TROJAN in Chapter 5).

Troy

A wealthy city on the east end of the Mediterranean, where the Trojan War was fought.

Turnus

The king of the Rutulians who was one of LAVINIA'S suitors and consequently battled against AENEAS for her. Turnus lost his life.

Tyche

The Greek name for the Goddess of Fortune.

Tydides

Another name for DIOMEDES.

Tyndaris

The daughter of Tyndareus and LEDA.

Tyro

The woman who bore POSEIDON twin sons, PELIAS and NELEUS.

Urania

The MUSE of Astronomy.

Uranis

One of ACTAEON'S hounds; the name means "heavenly one."

Uranus

The father of CRONUS, the TITANS, the CYCLOPS, and the Furies.

Venus

The Roman name for APHRODITE.

Vesper

Another name for HESPER.

Vesta

The Roman name for HESTIA.

Victoria

The Roman name for NIKE.

Virbius

The Roman name for HIPPOLYTUS.

Voluptas

The Roman Goddess of Pleasure.

Vulcan

The Roman name for HEPHAESTUS.

Xanthus

The gods' name for TROY'S great river.

Zephyr

The God of the West Wind.

Zetes

One of the ARGONAUTS.

Zethus

The twin brother of Amphion. Together, they built a wall around THEBES to fortify it.

"Moses"

7

Religious Names

This chapter contains names from the world's major religions. Most of the suggestions are from the Judeo-Christian tradition—particularly the Old and New Testaments; but many are derived from Hindu, Buddhist, or Islamic scriptures and related sources.

How About . . .

Adam

Cain

Eve

Malachi

Peter

Solomon

THE APOSTLES

Bartholomew
One of the Twelve Apostles, also known as NATHANAEL in one of the Gospels.

John
One of the Twelve Apostles. He is considered the author of Revelations and the Gospel of John.

Judas Iscariot
The Apostle who betrayed Jesus to His enemies.

Matthew
One of the Twelve Apostles whose original name was LEVI. The Gospel of Matthew is ascribed to him.

Nathanael
One of the Twelve Apostles, known as BARTHOLOMEW in the first three Gospels.

Peter
The Apostle who as a fisherman had been called SIMON (THE CANAANITE). Jesus changed his name to Peter, meaning "rock."

Philip
One of the Twelve Apostles.

Simon (the Canaanite)
One of the Twelve Apostles.

Thaddaeus
One of the Twelve Apostles. He is also called Jude and Lebbaeus.

FAMOUS/HISTORICAL RELIGIOUS FIGURES

Abraham
The founder of the Hebrew people.

Brahma
The supreme Hindu deity, called Creator of the Worlds.

Buddha (Guatama)
The founder of Buddhism, which holds that suffering is inherent in life but that one can rise beyond it by mental and moral self-purification.

"Buddha"

David

The boy who slew the giant GOLIATH and went on to become the greatest of Israel's kings. He built the city of Jerusalem.

Elijah

A great prophet of Israel who opposed AHAB and Queen JEZEBEL by fighting against the worship of the BAAL.

Gabriel

The archangel who announced the birth of Christ to the Virgin Mary (see MARY THE VIRGIN) and told her what to name Him.

Mary Magdalene

A woman who was one of Jesus's devoted followers. She was one of the two women who discovered Jesus's empty tomb.

Mary the Virgin

The mother of Jesus and wife of JOSEPH.

Solomon

King DAVID's son who became the third king of Israel and built the first temple.

MORE RELIGIOUS NAMES

Aaron

MOSES' brother whose rod became a serpent, when he cast it before Pharaoh. Aaron and his sons became the first priests of the Tabernacle.

Abednego

One of DANIEL'S three friends who survived the fiery furnace.

Abel

The son of ADAM and EVE. Abel's brother, CAIN, murdered him.

Absalom

A son of King DAVID who led a revolt against his father.

Adam

The first man created by God.

Agni

The Hindu fire god.

Ahab

The seventh king of the Northern Kingdom who married JEZEBEL. She persuaded him to abandon the worship of God for BAAL, the pagan deity.

Amalek

Esau's grandson who founded a warlike tribe that fought the Israelites.

Amos

A Hebrew prophet.

Ananias

An early Jewish Christian. When he and his wife lied to God, PETER denounced them, and they died.

Andrew

The brother of PETER who was one of the first disciples of Jesus.

Anna

A Hebrew prophetess who worshipped the infant Jesus.

Annas

The High Priest CAIAPHAS's father-in-law. When Jesus appeared before him after his arrest, Annas sent him to Caiaphas.

Antipas

One of Herod's sons who ruled Galilee and Perea during Jesus's lifetime. Antipas ordered JOHN THE BAPTIST beheaded.

Archelaus

One of Herod's sons who ruled Judea when JOSEPH (2), MARY (see MARY THE VIRGIN), and Jesus returned from Egypt.

Asenath

The wife of JOSEPH (1) who bore him two sons, Manasseh and EPHRAIM.

Baal

A pagan god worshiped in Phoenicia and Canaan whom some of the Israelites began to worship, angering God.

Barabbas

The robber whom PONTIUS PILATE released instead of Jesus.

Barak

The leader of Israel's forces against the Canaanite forces of King Jabin.

Barnabas

An early convert to Christianity who with PAUL preached the Gospel of Jesus.

Bartimaeus

A blind beggar whose faith in Jesus restored his sight.

Bast

The Egyptian Goddess of Matrimony and Feminine Sensuality. Bast was originally represented as a cat.

Beelzebub

A pagan god whom the Philistines worshipped. He is sometimes identified with Satan.

Belshazzar

The Babylonian ruler for whom DANIEL interpreted the significance of the handwriting on the wall.

Benjamin

The youngest of Jacob's and Rachel's twelve sons.

Boaz

RUTH's second husband to whom she bore a son named Obed.

Caiaphas

The High Priest, a friend of the Romans, who tried Jesus and then turned Him over to PONTIUS PILATE.

Cain

The first-born son of ADAM and EVE. He killed his brother, ABEL.

Caleb

MOSES' spy who reported on the Canaanites' strength.

Chilion

NAOMI's and ELIMELECH's son.

Chuza

The husband of JOANNA.

Cleopas

One of the two disciples with whom Jesus spoke on the way to Emmaus after the Resurrection.

Cornelius

A Roman centurion who saw a vision and then was baptized by PETER, thus becoming the first Gentile to convert to Christianity.

Cush

A son of HAM named after the land where his descendants lived.

Cyrus

The founder of the Persian Empire who released the Jews and told them to return to Jerusalem.

Dagon

One of the Philistines' pagan gods.

Dalai Lama

The spiritual leader of the Tibetan and Mongolian branch of Buddhism.

Daniel

Israel's great prophet whom God delivered from the lions' den.

Darius

The Babylonian king who cast DANIEL to the lions because of his great love for God.

Deborah

A prophetess who helped BARAK defeat the Canaanites.

Delilah

SAMSON'S love who betrayed him to the Philistines.

Demas

An early Christian who accompanied PAUL during his first Roman imprisonment.

Demetrius

A silversmith who incited a riot against PAUL because the latter's preaching had ruined the man's sale of silver models of the temple of the goddess Diana.

Dinah

A daughter of JACOB and Leah.

Dionysius

An Athenian whom PAUL converted and who became the first bishop of Athens.

Dorcas

Another name for Tabitha, a woman disciple whom PETER raised from the dead.

Drusilla

A daughter of Herod Agrippa I.

Eleazar

One of AARON'S sons who became High Priest after his father's death.

Eli

The priest at Shiloh. Hannah brought her son SAMUEL to him.

Elimelech

NAOMI'S husband and father of RUTH'S first husband, Mahlon.

Elisabeth

The mother of JOHN THE BAPTIST and a cousin of Mary (see MARY THE VIRGIN), the mother of Jesus.

Elisha

The prophet who succeeded ELIJAH.

Elkanah

The husband of HANNAH who was the father of the prophet SAMUEL.

Enoch

CAIN'S eldest son.

Epaenetus

The first Greek convert to Christianity.

Epaphras

An early Christian friend of PAUL.

Ephraim

JOSEPH'S second son. Part of Canaan was named for him.

Erastus

One of PAUL'S attendants who went as a missionary into Macedonia.

Esau

ISAAC'S eldest son who sold his birthright to his brother JACOB for a bowl of lentils.

Esther

A Hebrew orphan girl who married Ahasuerus (Xerxes), the King of Persia, and consequently was able to save her people from persecution.

Eutychus

A young man who fell from a window while listening to PAUL. The apostle restored his life.

Eve

The first woman created by God.

Ezekiel

A major Hebrew prophet.

Ezra

A Hebrew priest and scholar.

Felix

The Roman procurator who tried PAUL.

Gad

The son of JACOB and Zilpah who founded one of the Twelve Tribes of Israel.

Gedaliah

The Hebrew governor appointed by NEBUCHADNEZZAR.

Gehazi

The Prophet ELISHA's servant who was cursed with leprosy for betraying his master.

Gershon

One of the three grandsons of JACOB who accompanied him to Eygpt.

Gideon

One of the great judges of Israel, whom God chose to free the Children of Israel from the threat of the Midianites and other hostile tribes.

Goliath

The giant whom DAVID killed.

Habakkuk

A minor Hebrew prophet.

Hagar

SARAH's handmaid. She was the mother of ISHMAEL, who is regarded as the ancestor of the Arabs.

Haggai

A minor Hebrew prophet.

Ham

One of NOAH'S sons. Ham is considered the ancestor of all black Africans.

Hamutal

The mother of two kings—Jehoahaz and Zedekiah.

Hannah

The mother of SAMUEL, the judge and prophet.

Hanuman

The monkey god in Hindu mythology.

Heman

A musician and dancer and the grandson of the prophet SAMUEL. Heman sang and played in the temple during the reign of King DAVID.

Hephzibah

Wife of King HEZEKIAH. The name means "my delight is in her."

Herodias

Herod Antipas's wife who actually was instrumental in the death of JOHN THE BAPTIST.

Hezekiah

A king of Judah who reclaimed some of his nation's lands from the Philistines.

Hilkiah

A high priest who discovered the lost *Book of the Law*, or *Deuteronomy*.

Hophni

ELI'S son who, with his brother, died in battle, losing the Ark of the Covenant to the Philistines.

Hosea

A minor prophet.

Hur

A Hebrew who stood by MOSES during the battle with AMALEK.

Ichabod

The grandson of ELI.

Indra

The Hindu Rain God, the King of heaven.

Isaac

ABRAHAM's son whom Abraham almost sacrificed to God to prove his faith. Isaac married REBEKAH, and they had two sons, ESAU and JACOB.

Isaiah

Generally regarded as the greatest Hebrew prophet.

Ishmael

Abraham's son by HAGAR, his wife's handmaid. Ishmael founded a great nation of people in Arabia, where the Muslims revere him.

Israel

The name given to JACOB by an angel, which the Twelve Hebrew Tribes later adopted.

Jacob

Son of ISAAC and REBEKAH, who wrestled with the angel of the Lord and consequently was named ISRAEL.

Jambavat

The Hindu King of the Bears.

James

(1) The son of Alphaeus who became one of the Twelve Apostles. (2) The Apostle who was the son of ZEBEDEE and the brother of JOHN.

Jehoshaphat

One of JUDAH's greatest kings, who tried to abolish paganism and who was a great military leader.

Jeremiah

A major Hebrew prophet.

Jesse

King DAVID's father.

Jezebel

The evil queen married to King AHAB. She persecuted the Israelites until chariot horses trampled her to death.

Joanna

One of Jesus's earliest followers.

Job

A man who suffered a long series of great miseries. His name has become synonymous with patience.

John the Baptist

Jesus's forerunner.

Jonah

The Hebrew prophet who was swallowed by a whale because he did not want to go to Nineveh to preach. He repented and went to Nineveh.

Joseph

(1) One of JACOB's and RACHEL's sons. Joseph's jealous brothers sold him as a slave into Egypt. (2) The husband of Mary (see MARY THE VIRGIN), the mother of Jesus.

Joshua

An Israelite who after MOSES' death led his people in their first conquests in Canaan.

Judah

JACOB's fourth son who founded the largest of the Twelve Tribes of Israel.

OTHER DEITIES . . .	
Baal	Shiva
Bast	Varuna
Beelzebub	Vayu
Dagon	Vishnu
Saraswati	Yuma

Jude

The son of Mary (see MARY THE VIRGIN) and JOSEPH, thus believed by some to be a brother of Jesus.

Kama

The Hindu God of Love.

Kasmir (or Katmir or Kitmir)

The dog, according to Muslim tradition, that was one of the animals Mohammed admitted to Paradise.

Krishna

An incarnation of VISHNU.

Lazarus

Jesus's friend and the brother of MARTHA and MARY OF BETHANY. Jesus raised Lazarus from the dead.

Levi

One of JACOB's sons. Levi founded one of the Twelve Tribes of Israel.

Lot

ABRAHAM'S nephew whom God saved, along with his family, from the destruction of Sodom.

Lucifer

The light-bearer; the star that brings in the day (the morning star). Originally an archangel, Lucifer led a rebellion, was cast out of heaven, and became identified with the Devil.

Luke

An early Christian who accompanied PAUL on two of his missionary journeys. The third gospel is attributed to Luke.

Lydia

A wealthy woman who was PAUL's first European convert.

Malachi

A prophet of Israel.

Mark

One of the Evangelists. He is considered the author of the *Gospel of Mark*.

Martha

The sister of LAZARUS and MARY OF BETHANY.

Mary of Bethany

The sister of MARTHA and LAZARUS, who anointed Jesus in Simon the Leper's house.

Matthias

The disciple chosen to take the place of JUDAS.

Mecca

The birthplace of MOHAMMED in Saudi Arabia and the Islamic holy city.

Meshach

One of DANIEL'S three companions who survived the fiery furnace.

Methuselah

A Biblical figure who was renowned for his longevity.

Meuzza

Mohammed's beloved cat. She was one of the animals admitted to Islamic Paradise.

Micah

A minor Hebrew prophet.

Miriam

MOSES and AARON's sister who became a prophetess.

Moses

The Hebrew prophet who led the Israelites out of Egypt and who received the Ten Commandments from God.

Naomi

The mother-in-law of RUTH.

Nebuchadnezzar

A powerful king of Babylon who invaded Israel several times, carrying its people into bondage and razing Jerusalem and the Holy Temple.

Nicodemus

A Pharisee who defended Jesus at one of His trials, and buried Him after the Crucifixion.

Noah

The builder of the ark who saved himself, his family, and two of each of the world's animals from the Flood.

Obadiah

A minor prophet.

Obed

The grandfather of King DAVID.

Paul

The first Christian missionary who had persecuted Christians until he saw a vision on the road to Damascus.

Pontius Pilate

The Roman procurator of Judea who tried and condemned Jesus.

Ra

The Eygptian God of the Sun.

Rachel

The wife of JACOB and mother of his sons, JOSEPH and BENJAMIN.

Rama

The Hindu king who was the son of VISHNU, his incarnation on earth.

Ravan

The Hindu demon king.

Rebekah

The wife of ABRAHAM's son ISAAC and mother of his sons, ESAU and JACOB.

Reuben

JACOB's first son who founded one of the Twelve Tribes of Israel.

Ruth

The young woman whose story is told in the Old Testament *Book of Ruth*. She was the great-grandmother of King DAVID.

Samson

The strongest man in the Bible who received his strength from his long hair. His love, DELILAH, betrayed him.

BIBLICAL CHARACTERS . . .	
Abel	Eve
Adam	Isaiah
Ahab	Lazarus
Cain	Samuel
Eli	

Samuel

A prophet and judge of Israel who delivered the Israelites at Mizpah from Philistine oppression and who anointed SAUL as the first king of Israel.

Sarah

The wife of ABRAHAM.

Sarama

The great god INDRA'S watchdog and messenger in Hindu mythology.

Sarameyau

SARAMA's savage twin sons in Hindu mythology, who guided the souls of the dead to their final resting place.

Saraswati

The Hindu Goddess of Speech.

Saul

The first king of Israel.

Seth

The third son of ADAM and EVE.

Shadrach

One of DANIEL'S three companions who survived the fiery furnace.

Sheba (Queen of)

The wealthy queen who visited King SOLOMON.

Shiva

The great Hindu god whose third eye will destroy the world.

Simeon

A son of JACOB and LEAH, who founded one of the Twelve Tribes of Israel.

Simon of Cyrene

The man who carried the cross for Jesus.

Sita

RAMA's wife, the ideal Hindu woman.

Stephen

An early Christian. He was stoned to death for his beliefs, thereby becoming the first Christian martyr.

Thomas

The Apostle known as "doubting Thomas" because he would not believe in the Resurrection until he saw Jesus's wounds.

Timothy

PAUL's friend and companion.

Titus

PAUL's Greek assistant and companion, who was converted by him.

Tobit's Dog

(1) One of the animals placed in Islamic Paradise. (2) The dog who appears in the *Book of Tobit* in the Apocrypha to the Bible.

Varuna

The Hindu God of the Waters.

Vayu

The Hindu God of the Wind.

Vishnu

The great Hindu god who preserves the three worlds.

Yama

The Hindu God of Death.

Zacharias

A priest who was the father of JOHN THE BAPTIST.

Zebedee

The father of the two apostles JAMES and JOHN.

Zechariah (or Zachariah)

A priest and minor Hebrew prophet whose visions and teachings appear in the Old Testament that bears his name.

Zephaniah

A minor prophet of Israel whose teachings appear in the Old Testament named for him.

Zoroaster

A Persian religious teacher, the founder of the Zoroastrian religion.

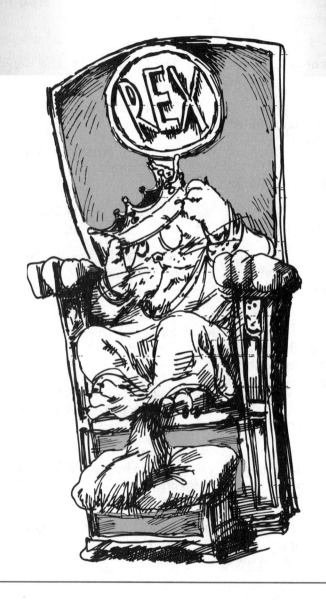

Royalty and Titles

There is no better way to exalt your pet and show your high esteem than by giving it a prestigious title. Most of the names in this section are royal designations, but quite a few are derived from military or civil terms.

How About . . .

BARON

CAPTAIN

LADY

LORD

MR. PRESIDENT

QUEENIE

SIR KNIGHT

Royalty and Titles

Admiral

Airman

Ambassador

Baron

Baroness

Barrister

Brigadier
  (General)

Brother

Cadet

Captain

Chancellor

Chief

Coach

Colonel

Commander

Corporal

Counselor

Count

Countess

Czar (Tsar)

Czarina (Tsarina)

Dean

Detective

Director

Doctor

Duchess

Duke

Earl

Emperor

Empress

Ensign

General

Gladiator

Governor

Highness

Inspector

Judge

Kaiser

Khan

King

Knight

Lady

Leader

Lieutenant

Lord

Madame

Mademoiselle

Maestro

Majesty

Major

"Pasha"

Master	Pasha	Rabbi	Señorita
Matriarch	Patriarch	Representative	Sergeant
Mayor	Pharaoh	Reverend	Shah
Midshipman	Preacher	Rex	Sheik
Minister	Premier	Rey	Shogun
Miss	President	Ruler	Sir
Mister	Prime Minister	Seaman	Sister
Mistress	Prince	Secretary	Soldier
Monsieur	Princess	Senator	Squire
Ms.	Private	Senior	Teacher
Officer	Queen/Queenie	Señor	

LEADERS OF THE WORLD

Chancellor	Kaiser
Chief	King
Czar	Premier
Emperor	President
Empress	Prime Minister
General	Queen

"McDuff"

Foreign Words and Names

If you have a flair for the exotic or simply want to impress your friends with your linguistic skills, then the names in this chapter will intrigue you (and possibly prompt you to open a foreign language dictionary!). Your best choice is a pleasant sounding word, preferably one you can pronounce correctly, and one with a translation that appropriately fits your pet. For instance, be careful not to embarrass yourself and your black cat by naming him Amarillo, the Spanish word for "yellow"!

How About . . .

Agape	Ilsa
Astra	Luna
Beau	Madame
Diablo	Rosita

Abogado

Spanish for "lawyer."

Agape

Greek for word meaning "love."

Allegre

Spanish for "happy."

Aloha

Hawaiian word for "hello" or "goodbye."

Amarillo(a)

Spanish for "yellow." Use Amarillo for a male and Amarilla for a female.

Amigo(a)

Spanish word meaning "friend." Use Amigo for a male and Amiga for a female.

Amore

Italian for "love."

Astra

Latin for "star."

Azul

Spanish for "blue."

Beau/Belle

French for "handsome/beautiful" (male/female).

Bébé

French for "baby."

Beeren

German for "berries."

Bello(a)

Italian for "pretty."

Bianca Pinjarra

Some of the crown jewels of England.

Bianco(a)

Italian for "white." Use Bianco for a male and Bianca for a female.

Bier

German word for "beer."

Bijou

French for "jewel."

Blanco(a)

Spanish for "white." Use Blanco for a male and Blanca for a female.

Blanquito(a)

Spanish for "little white one." Use Blanquito for a male and Blanquita for a female.

Bleu/Bleue

French for "blue" (male/female).

Bobae

Korean for "heirloom."

Boca

Spanish for "mouth."

Bonito(a)

Spanish for "pretty." Use Bonito for a male and Bonita for a female.

Canela

Spanish for "cinnamon."

Caro/Cara

Italian for "dear" (male/female). Gaelic for "friend."

Celia

"Little heavenly one."

Chansu

Japanese for "chance."

Chat

French for "cat."

Chatool

Hebrew for "cat."

Chico

Spanish for "young man."

Chien

French for "dog."

Chiquita

Spanish for "little girl."

Cinco

Spanish for "five."

Coeur

French for "heart."

Concha

Spanish for "shell."

Deja Vu

French for "already seen."

Diablo

Spanish for "devil."

Diez

Spanish for "ten."

Dolce

Italian for "sweet."

Dono

Italian for "gift."

Dos

Spanish for "two."

Faeden

Gaelic for "golden."

Faux Pas

French for "a social blunder."

Felice

Italian for "happy."

Feliz

Spanish for "happy."

Feo

Spanish for "ugly."

Foreign Words and Names

Fiesta
Spanish for "party."

Flavo
Italian for "fair or blonde."

Fraulein
German for "young woman."

Freida
A German name for a female.

Frieden
German for "peace."

Frijol
Spanish for "bean."

Fritz
A German name for a male.

Gato(a)
Spanish for "cat." Use *Gato* for a male and *Gata* for a female.

Gigio
Italian for "cricket."

Greta
A German name for a female.

Gretchen
A German name for a female.

Gretel
A German name for a female.

"Fiesta"

Gris
Spanish for "gray."

Hans
A German name for a male.

Heidi
A German name for a female.

Heinrich
A German name for a male; it translates as "Henry."

Hombre
Spanish for "man."

Hummel
A German name for a male.

Ilsa
A German name for a female.

José
A Spanish name for a male.

Kannika
"Jasmine-like blossom" in Japanese.

Katarina (Katrina)
A Russian name for a female.

Keseff
Hebrew for "silver."

Klein
German for "small."

Kochka
Russian for "cat."

Koyuki
Japanese for "snow."

Kui
Hawaiian for "roar."

Kut
The Egyptian name for the male cat.

Kutta
The Egyptian name for the female cat.

Laddie
Scottish for "young man."

Lassie
Scottish for "young woman."

Lieb
German for "dear."

Liesel
A German name for a female.

Linda
Spanish for "pretty."

Luna
Spanish for "moon."

Madame
French for "Mrs. or Madam."

Mademoiselle
French for "Miss."

Mar
Spanish for "sea."

Marta
A German name for a female.

McCloud
A Scottish name.

McDuff
A Scottish name.

McMurphy
A Scottish name.

McTavish
A Scottish name.

Mesa
Spanish for "table."

Mi
Spanish for "my."

Misha
A Russian name for a male.

Monique
A French name for a female.

Monsieur
French for "Mister."

Muñeca
Spanish for "doll."

Natasha
A Russian name for a female.

Nicole
A French name for a female.

Nikko
Japanese for "cat."

Nueve
Spanish for "nine."

Ocho
Spanish for "eight."

Octavia/n
A Latin name for a female/male.

Omar
A Middle Eastern name.

Oso(a)
Spanish for "bear." Use Oso for a male and Osa for a female.

Paco
A Spanish name for a male.

Pancho
A Spanish name for a male.

Pepe
A Spanish name for a male.

Perro(a)
Spanish for "dog." Use Perro for a male and Perra for a female.

Poco
Spanish for "little."

Quatro
Spanish for "four."

Renée
A French name.

Rio
Spanish for "river."

Rojo(a)
Spanish for "red." Use Rojo for a male and Roja for a female.

Rosita
A Spanish name for a female.

Sasha
A Russian name.

Sayonara
Japanese for "goodbye."

Schnell
German for "fast" or "quick."

Schotzie
A German name.

Seis
Spanish for "six."

Señor
Spanish for "Mister."

Señorita
Spanish for "Miss."

Siete
Spanish for "seven."

Simba
African for "lion."

Som Phong
Tai word meaning "like one's ancestors."

Suki
A Japanese name.

Summa
Latin for "the most."

Sushi
Japanese for "raw fish."

Taiko
Japanese for "boss."

Tanya
A Russian name for a female.

Tasha
A Russian female name. (Short for Natasha.)

Tia
Spanish for "aunt."

Tigre(a)
Spanish for "tiger." Use Tigre for a male and Tigra for a female.

Tio
Spanish for "uncle."

Toro
Spanish for "bull."

Toutou
French for "doggie."

Tres
Spanish for "three."

Trinka
A German name for a female. (Short for Katrinka.)

Uno
Spanish for "one."

Vaquero
Spanish for "cowboy."

Wolfgang
A German name for a male.

"Puss in Boots"

10

Literature and Art

Some of the most memorable animals are those that appear in literature and art. This chapter includes many of those animals, particularly dogs and cats, as well as a few famous human literary and artistic characters.

How About . . .

Atticus Finch

Iago

Mr. Darcy

Romeo

Elizabeth Bennet

Shakespeare

Gandalf

FAMOUS LITERARY HEROES

Atticus Finch
Valiant lawyer and central character in Harper Lee's *To Kill a Mockingbird*.

"Atticus Finch"

Beowulf
The hero of the Anglo-Saxon epic poem *Beowulf*.

Bond (James)
The main character and British spy in the popular Ian Fleming fictional series.

King Arthur
The legendary king of the Britons who restored order and peace in his kingdom. King Arthur's story is told in various literary works.

Sherlock Holmes
The famous detective in Sir Arthur Conan Doyle's (1859–1930) books.

FAMOUS LITERARY VILLAINS

Caliban
A character in the Shakespearean play *The Tempest*.

Iago
Most famous Shakespeare villain. The villainous Iago, who drives the title character to madness and murder, is from SHAKESPEARE'S *Othello*.

Professor Moriarity
The arch enemy of Sherlock Holmes in Sir Arthur Conan Doyle's (1859–1930) mystery books.

"Voldemort"

Nazgul

Ringwraiths. Seven kings of men who fell and now work in service of Sauron in *The Lord of the Rings*.

Sauron

The great eye and the Lord of the Rings, from J.R.R. Tolkien's *The Lord of the Rings*.

Voldemort

The evil wizard in the *Harry Potter* series.

FAMOUS ANIMALS IN LITERATURE

Aslan

A powerful lion who can see into the future and guides the children who visit Narnia to victory in *The Chronicles of Narnia* series.

Charlotte

A spider, the title character in *Charlotte's Web* by E. B. White. She saves the life of WILBUR the pig.

Cheshire Cat, The

The famous grinning cat whom Alice encounters during her journey in *Alice's Adventures in Wonderland* (1865) by Lewis Carroll. (See also *Cheshire Cat* in Chapter 11.)

Clifford

Title character of Norman Bridwell's children's book, *Clifford the Big Red Dog*.

Mittens

The kitten who laughed so hard she fell off the wall in Beatrix Potter's *The Tale of Tom Kitten*.

Old Yeller

The rugged, stray yellow-gold dog who was adopted in Fred Gipson's *Old Yeller*, a novel about the Texas hill country in the frontier days of the 1860s. Old Yeller's name had a double meaning: the color of his hair coat and the yelling sounds he made.

SOME FAMOUS WRITERS

Agatha Christie

The famous twentieth-century mystery writer.

Chaucer (Geoffrey)

The greatest English poet of the Middle Ages who is best known for his classic, *The Canterbury Tales*.

Dante

One of the greatest medieval poets. Dante's major literary work was *The Divine Comedy*.

Dickens (Charles)

One of the most popular English novelists who criticized the wealthy and corrupt in nineteenth-century England.

Frost (Robert)

One of America's greatest twentieth-century poets and winner of the Pulitzer Prize in 1924, 1931, 1937, and 1943 (1874–1965).

Homer

The blind poet who wrote of the Greek myths in *The Iliad* and *The Odyssey*.

MORE NAMES FROM LITERATURE AND ART

Adonis

Title character in the Shakespearean narrative poem *Venus and Adonis*.

Aladdin

The boy hero who releases a magic genie by rubbing a magic lamp in *The Thousand and One Nights*.

Alidoro

A mastiff in Carlos Collodi's (Lorenzini) *Pinocchio* (1883). Pinocchio saved Alidoro from drowning; in return Alidoro rescued the puppet from being fried like a fish when coated with flour.

Ann

One of the bluetick hounds of the pair Ann and DAN in the book *Where the Red Fern Grows* by Wilson Rawls.

Antony (Mark)

(Marcus Antonius, 83?–30 B.C.) Triumvir in Rome with Octavian and Marcus Aemilius Lepidus after the murder of Julius Caesar. Also a character in the Shakespearean plays *Antony and Cleopatra* and *Julius Caesar*.

Appollinaris

A cat that belonged to Mark Twain.

Aragorn

King of Gondor and member of the Fellowship of the Ring. From *The Lord of the Rings*.

Ariel

A delicate spirit in the Shakespearean play *The Tempest*.

Aristophanes

A Greek comedy writer during the last half of the fifth and first half of the fourth centuries B.C. He refers to the myths in his works.

Ashley

The master of Twelve Oaks in Margaret Mitchell's classic novel *Gone With the Wind* (1936).

Aurora

A character from Jimmy Buffett's *Tales from Margaritaville*.

Banshee

A female spirit in Gaelic folklore whose appearance or wailing warns a family of the approaching death of one of its members.

Barge

In *The Fireside Book of Dog Stories* (1943), James Thurber tells of Barge, a watchdog who lived with a family in Columbus, Ohio. Barge took to drinking and neglected his duties until he came home one day and found that burglars had broken into his house. In despair and shame, Barge jumped out of a window and killed himself.

Baron

A dachshund in the book *Park Avenue Vet*, written by Louis J. Camuti.

Basket

Gertrude Stein's two dogs of the same name. They are described in works that Stein wrote in France during the period of the German occupation (1940–1945).

Belgarath

Disciple of Aldur and protector of the Rivan King in David Eddings' *The Belgariad*.

Bella Swan

Main character in the *Twilight* book series. Falls in love with Edward Cullen, a local vampire, after moving to a new town.

Ben

A dog described by Maxwell Knight, in *My Pet Friends*.

Bevis

A large hound that was a prominent figure in Sir Walter Scott's novel *Woodstock* and was characterized after his own Scottish deerhound.

Big Red

The $7,000 Irish setter in Jim Kjelgaard's *Big Red* (1945). Big Red ruined his chances to be a show dog when he injured himself fighting a wolverine and a bear, thereby saving his master Danny Pickett.

Bilbo Baggins

One of the hobbits in J.R.R. Tolkien's novels.

Bion

An Alexandrian pastoral poet who wrote of the myths, around 250 B.C.

Blackie

A black spaniel that was Ernest Hemingway's companion for twelve years.

Blanche

One of the dogs that does not appear on stage but is mentioned in Act 3, Scene 6 of SHAKESPEARE'S play *King Lear* (1608).

Boatswain

Lord Byron's Newfoundland and the subject of a moving epitaph by the well-known poet.

Bodger

The old bull terrier in Sheila Burnford's *The Incredible Journey* (1961). Bodger was one of the three pets who faced tremendous hardships while traveling home through the Canadian wilderness.

Boring Alice

A character from Jimmy Buffett's *Tales from Margaritaville*.

Brownie

The female Irish setter owned by T. H. White, the author of *The Once and Future King* (1958). White described his love for Brownie in his letters to David Garnett.

Buck

The large, powerful, mix-breed dog in Jack London's *The Call of the Wild*. Stolen from his home in California to be sold as a sled dog in Alaska, Buck was "beaten but not broken." He eventually joined a pack of wolves who signaled their acceptance of Buck by sniffing noses and howling at the moon.

Bull's-eye

The white shaggy mutt in Charles Dickens's *Oliver Twist* (1839). Bull's-eye belonged to the murderer, Bill Sikes, and had as unpleasant a disposition as his owner.

Bunyan (Paul)

The mythical lumberjack hero of the American West.

Cadpig

The smallest and prettiest of Pongo's fifteen puppies in Dodie Smith's *The Hundred and One Dalmatians* (1956). Cadpig's favorite pastime is watching television.

Caesar (Julius)

The powerful Roman political and military leader (100–44 B.C.) who was eventually murdered by Brutus. Appears in Shakespeare's play *Julius Caesar*.

Catarina

A large tortoiseshell cat that belonged to Edgar Allan Poe and his wife Virginia. Catarina would lie on Virginia to keep her warm when Virginia was bedridden.

Catfish

Columnist Lewis Grizzard's dog who, as Grizzard reports in his column, liked to drink out of the toilet.

Caulfield (Holden)

Unpredictable main character in *The Catcher in the Rye*.

Charley

The large French poodle that accompanied John Steinbeck on his trip through the United States in the 1960s. Steinbeck recalls their adventures in *Travels with Charley* in which Charley is described as being his ambassador when meeting strange people.

Cinderella

The girl who marries Prince Charming in the well-known fairy tale *Cinderella*.

Clarissa

A dog in James Thurber's *How to Name a Dog*.

Columbine

A stock character in early Italian comedy and pantomime. Columbine was the daughter of Pantaloon and the sweetheart of HARLEQUIN.

Cotton-Tail

The brother of FLOPSY and MOPSY. These three were the "good little bunnies [who] went down to the lane to gather blackberries," from Beatrix Potter's *The Tale of Peter Rabbit*.

Cujo

The canine title character of a Stephen KING novel.

Cullen (Edward)

Vampire love and protector of Bella Swan in the *Twilight* book series.

da Vinci (Leonardo)

The renowned Italian painter, artist, sculptor, and architect (1452–1519).

"da Vinci"

Damn Spot

From SHAKESPEARE'S *Macbeth* (published in 1623), in which Lady Macbeth proclaimed: "Out, out, Damn spot" while walking through the castle distraught over the blood on her garment after killing King Duncan.

Dan

Half of the pair ANN and Dan in the book *Where the Red Fern Grows*.

Darcy, Mr.

Love interest of Elizabeth Bennet in Jane Austen's *Pride and Prejudice*.

Dash

A mongrel dog that belonged to writer Charles Lamb. Dash had once belonged to poet Thomas Hood. Lamb wrote about Dash's "crazy" behavior, which included the ability to stand on his hind legs.

FANTASTIC FANTASY	
Aragorn	Oz
Belgarath	Polgara
Bella Swan	Sinbad
Bilbo Baggins	Snape
Cullen	Tolkien
Dumbledore	Toto
Gandalf	

Dash

Dashiell Hammett (1894–1961), an American crime novelist whose works include *The Maltese Falcon* and *The Thin Man*.

Digit

A gorilla in the book *Gorillas in the Mist* by Diane Fosse (1983). He got his name from the fourth and fifth digits of his hand, which were webbed.

Dinah

Alice's cat, who was left behind when Alice fell down the rabbit-hole in Lewis Carroll's *Alice's Adventures in Wonderland* (1865).

Diogenes

The brutish dog that adored his owner, Florence Dombey, in Charles Dickens's *Dombey and Son* (1848).

Don Juan

One of the most famous literary figures in medieval legends. Don Juan has appeared in the works of Byron, Shaw, Moliere, and Mozart.

Dr. Watson

Sherlock Holmes's companion and the narrator of Sir Arthur Conan Doyle's (1859–1930) mystery books.

Duke

Penrod Schofield's dog. A scraggly, but faithful, companion in Booth Tarkington's *Penrod* (1914). (See also DUKE in Chapter 5.)

Dumbledore

The wise wizard and headmaster of Hogwarts in the *Harry Potter* series.

El Dorado

The fictitious kingdom of untold wealth on the Amazon River for which Spanish and English explorers searched.

Elizabeth Bennet

The heroine who falls in love with the elusive Mr. Darcy in Jane Austen's *Pride and Prejudice*.

Emerson (Ralph Waldo)

American poet, essayist, and lecturer (1803–1882).

Euripides

A Greek tragic poet of the fifth century B.C., who wrote plays based on myths.

Feathers

Carl van Vechten's cat, whose behavior he discussed in *The Tiger in the House* (1920).

Flicka

The title character in a novel about a horse, entitled *My Friend Flicka*.

Flopsy

One of the "good little bunnies" in Beatrix Potter's stories. (See COTTON-TAIL.)

Flossy

English writer Anne Bronte's fat little black-and-white spaniel.

Flush

Elizabeth Barrett Browning's red cocker spaniel. Elizabeth was holding Flush when she met Robert in Hodgson's Bookshop in 1846.

Fortitude

One of two lions whose statues guard the Fifth Avenue entrance to the main building of the New York Public Library. (See PATIENCE.)

Foss

Edward Lear's beloved tomcat for whom he created "The Heraldic Blazon of Foss the Cat," published in *Nonsense Songs, Stories, Botany and Alphabets*.

Fu Manchu

The villain in Sax Rohmer novels.

Gandalf

A wizard sent to Middle-Earth to monitor Sauron and protect the world. From *The Lord of the Rings*.

Gatsby (Jay)

A racketeer of the 1920s in F. Scott Fitzgerald's classic novel *The Great Gatsby* (1925).

Gipsy

The cat who left home to become an alley cat in Booth Tarkington's *Penrod and Sam*.

Goldilocks

The little girl in the children's fairy tale *The Three Bears*.

Grendel

An anthropomorphic monster who ravaged Herot for twelve years and was killed by BEOWULF in the novel *Beowulf*.

Grimalkin

The demon spirit in the form of a cat mentioned by the First Witch in SHAKESPEARE'S *Macbeth* (1605).

Guinevere

KING ARTHUR'S wife in the stories of *King Arthur and the Round Table*.

Gulliver

Title character in Jonathan Swift's
Gulliver's Travels (1726).

Hamlet

Title character of a Shakespearean play,
believed to be written in 1603.

Harlequin

A clown in early Italian comedy and
pantomime. Harlequin's tight-fitting
costume has alternating patches of
contrasting colors.

Hank the Cowdog

Title character of a children's book series
by John R. Erikson.

Harry Potter

The powerful teen wizard who is destined
to fight Lord Voldemort in the bestselling
Harry Potter series by J.K. Rowling.

Heidi

The heroine of *Heidi* by Johanna Spyri
(1827–1901).

Hemingway (Ernest)

American novelist (1899–1961), 1954
winner of the Nobel Prize. Wrote *The Sun
Also Rises*, *A Farewell to Arms*, *The Old
Man and The Sea*, and *The Snows of
Kilimanjaro*, among others.

"Harry Potter"

Herodotus

The first historian of Europe. He refers to
the myths in his works.

Hinse

The cat that belonged to the poet and
novelist Sir Walter Scott of Edinburgh
(1771–1832).

Horatio

Character in the Shakespearean play *Hamlet*.

Hound of the Baskervilles, The

The ghostly black hound that dwelt on the moors of Dartmoor and terrorized the Baskerville family in Sir Arthur Conan Doyle's *The Hound of the Baskervilles* (1902).

Jack

Title character in the Mother Goose nursery rhyme "Jack and Jill."

Jeannie

A Scotty that appears in *Thurber's Dogs* (1955).

Jennie

The discontented Sealyham terrier that became the star of the World Mother Goose Theatre in Maurice Sendak's *Higglety Pigglety Pop! or There Must Be More to Life* (1967).

Jill

Title character in the Mother Goose nursery rhyme "Jack and Jill."

Jip

(1) Dora Spenlow's small black spaniel who liked to walk on the dinner table in Charles Dickens's *David Copperfield*

(1850). (2) The dog with an acute sense of smell that helped save a man stranded on an island in Hugh Lofting's *The Story of Doctor Dolittle* (1920).

Juliet

One of the star-crossed lovers in SHAKESPEARE'S *Romeo and Juliet* (1594–1595).

Keeper

Emily Brontë's mastiff. When his mistress died, Keeper followed the coffin in the funeral procession and slept for nights at the door of her empty room.

Kiche

The she-wolf who whelped in Jack London's *White Fang* (1906).

King (Stephen)

A contemporary author of horror books, including *Carrie*, *The Shining*, *Pet Sematary*, and *The Dead Zone*.

Kipling (Rudyard)

English poet, short story writer, and novelist (1865–1936); wrote *The Light That Failed* and *The Jungle Book*, as well as the well-known poem *Gunga Din*, among other works.

Lad

The thoroughbred collie who accomplished amazing deeds in Albert Payson Terhune's *Lad: A Dog* (1919). Terhune based Lad on his own collie, Sunnybank Lad.

Lady Godiva

The wife of Loefric, Earl of Mercia and Lord of Coventry. She rode naked through the town to get her husband to lower heavy taxes on the people (c.1040–1080).

Lancelot

Sir Lancelot du Lac, the best of KING ARTHUR'S knights, who loved Arthur's wife GUINEVERE in the stories of *King Arthur and the Round Table*.

Lassie

The collie in Eric Knight's pre-World War II short story "Lassie Come Home" (1938), who has since become a symbol of loyalty and dignity.

Lion of Lucerne, The (Lowendenkmal)

A statue of a dying lion erected in Lucerne's Glacier Garden to commemorate the Swiss Guards who were killed defending Louis XVI during the French Revolution.

Lobo

The "King of Currumpaw," leader of a pack of wolves that attacked cattle in New Mexico. Ernest Thompson Seton wrote of his attempts to capture Lobo in *Wild Animals I Have Known* (1898). Seton finally succeeded by luring the wolf with the dead body of his mate, Blanca.

Longfellow (Henry Wadsworth)

The most popular and accomplished poet of the nineteenth century (1807–1882).

Lucian

A second-century A.D. Greek writer who satirized the gods.

Lysander

Character in the Shakespearean play *A Midsummer Night's Dream*.

Macavity

The ginger cat that mysteriously disappears whenever anything turns up missing in "Macavity: the Mystery Cat" from *Old Possum's Book of Practical Cats* (1939) by T. S. Eliot.

Macbeth

Title character of a Shakespearean play.

Marcellus
Character in the Shakespearean play *Hamlet*.

Max
A dachshund that is mentioned by Matthew Arnold in the elegy "Poor Matthias" (1882). See also MORITZ.

Merrylegs
Jupe's performing circus dog in Charles Dickens's *Hard Times* (1854) who disappeared with his owner, only to return to the circus alone, lame, and almost blind.

Meyer (Stephenie)
Author of the best-selling *Twilight* Saga.

Michelangelo
The immensely talented Florentine painter, sculptor, architect, and poet (1475–1564) who was known for, among other things, his painting of the ceiling of the Sistine Chapel in Rome.

Minnaloushe
A black cat that is the subject of three verses in William Butler Yeats's *The Cat and the Moon* (1919).

Miss Muffet
The girl frightened by a spider in the popular nursery rhyme.

Mistigris
Madame Vauquer's cat in Honore de Balzac's *Le Père Goriot* (1835).

Mona Lisa
Leonardo Da Vinci's famous painting of the woman with the mysterious smile.

Monsieur Tibault
The cat that conducted a symphony orchestra with his tail in Stephen Vincent Benét's *The King of the Cats* (1929).

Moppet
One of the two kittens that "trod upon their pinafores and fell on their noses," in Beatrix Potter's *The Tale of Tom Kitten*.

Mopsy
One of the "good little bunnies" in Beatrix Potter's stories. (See COTTON-TAIL.)

Moritz
From *Max and Moritz*, the German classic by Wilhelm Busch. The names designate a pair of mischief-makers.

Morris
The famous finicky, striped tomcat of 9-Lives Cat Food commercials whose biography was written by Mary Daniels in 1974.

Mouschi

A cat that belonged to Ann Frank as described in *Diary of a Young Girl*.

Mozart (Wolfgang Amadeus)

Austrian composer who began to write music at the age of five. He wrote more than forty symphonies and twenty-two operas, among other great musical works.

Muggs

(1) The ferocious airedale in James Thurber's "The Dog That Bit People" from *My Life and Hard Times* (1933). (2) One of James Thurber's dogs included in his book, *Thurber's Dogs* (1955).

Music

The female greyhound described by William Wordsworth in the poem, "Incident Characteristic of a Favorite Dog" (1805). Music, who belonged to Mrs. Wordsworth's brother, tried desperately to save her friend Dart who had fallen through the ice on a lake. As she was breaking away the ice with her paws, Wordsworth described the scene: "...For herself she hath no fears/Him alone she sees and hears."

Mutt

An amusing, black-and-white mongrel in Farley Mowat's *The Dog Who Wouldn't Be* (1957).

Nana

The Newfoundland dog that is the Darling children's nurse in J. M. Barrie's *Peter Pan* (1904).

Narnia

A magical land that the main characters in C.S. Lewis's *The Chronicles of Narnia* can enter through a wardrobe.

Nero

Jane Welsh Carlyle's white terrier, part Maltese and part mongrel, who one day jumped from the library window, knocking himself senseless. Virginia Woolf relates the incident, claiming that perhaps the dog was attempting suicide, in *Flush* (1933).

Nox

The big black retriever whose behavior helped Father Brown solve Colonel Druce's murder in G. K. Chesterton's "The Oracle of the Dog" from *The Incredulity of Father Brown* (1926).

Octavian (Augustus)

Julius Caesar's great-nephew (63 B.C.– A.D. 14).

Old Bob

The gray collie that was an award-winning sheepherder in *Bob, Son of Battle* (1898) by Alfred Ollivant.

Old Dan

A redbone hunting hound from the novel *Where the Red Fern Grows*.

Oliver (Twist)

The orphan in Charles Dickens's novel *Oliver Twist* (1837–39).

Othello

Title character of a Shakespearean play published in 1622.

Ovid

A Latin narrative poet who retold almost all of the stories of classical mythology.

Oz

From the novel *The Wonderful Wizard of Oz* (1900) by L. Frank Baum about Dorothy, a Kansas farm girl who was swept away by a tornado to the land of Oz.

Patience

One of two lions whose statues guard the Fifth Avenue entrance to the main building of the New York Public Library. (See FORTITUDE.)

Pepper

The names of three of Dandie Dinmont's six terriers (the other three were named MUSTARD) in Sir Walter Scott's *Guy Mannering* (1815).

Peter Rabbit

The mischievous little rabbit in Beatrix Potter's *The Tale of Peter Rabbit*. When Peter was hiding under a flower pot, he sneezed and was discovered by Mr. McGregor.

Phoebe

Holden's sister in J. D. Salinger's novel *The Catcher in the Rye* (1951).

Picasso (Pablo)

Famous Spanish artist and sculptor (1881–1973); the leading figure in modern art.

Pindar

Greece's greatest lyric poet who alludes to the myths in all his poems.

Pinocchio

The puppet whose nose grew when he lied in *Pinocchio* (1883) by Carlos Collodi (Lorenzini).

Polgara

Daughter of Belgarath the Sorcerer and guardian of the Rivan Kings in David Eddings' *The Belgariad*.

Prynne (Hester)

The main character in Nathaniel Hawthorne's 1850 novel *The Scarlet Letter*.

Puck

A character in the Shakespearean play *A Midsummer Night's Dream*.

Puss in Boots

The clever cat that was the sole inheritance a poor boy received from his father. The cat, who asked only for a pair of boots, tricked an ogre by challenging him to turn himself into a mouse. The cat ate the ogre, and his master took over the ogre's lands and castle.

Pyramus

A character in the Shakespearean play *A Midsummer Night's Dream*.

Rab

The powerful dog in Dr. John Brown's *Rab and His Friends* that kept a vigil at the bedside of his owner Ailie during her illness and subsequent death.

Raksha

The Mother Wolf that raised Mowgli in Rudyard Kipling's *The Jungle Book* (1894).

Rembrandt

A Dutch Baroque painter (1606–1669) whose works, including *The Night Watch*, have become treasured masterpieces.

Remus (Uncle)

The narrator of a series of stories by Joel Chandler Harris (1848–1908). Uncle Remus was a former slave who became a beloved family servant and who entertains a young boy by telling him animal stories.

Rhett

Rhett Butler, the irreverent Southerner who becomes Scarlett's third husband in Margaret Mitchell's *Gone With the Wind* (1936).

Rikki-Tikki-Tavi

The title character in RUDYARD KIPLING'S short story about a mongoose that fights cobras.

Rinnie

Nickname for *Rin Tin Tin*. (See Chapter 11.)

Romeo

One of the star-crossed lovers in SHAKESPEARE'S *Romeo and Juliet* (1594–1595).

Rum Tum Tugger

A fictional cat in *Old Possum's Book of Practical Cats* by T. S. Eliot (1939).

Salinger (J. D.)

An American author (b. 1919), best known for his novel *The Catcher in the Rye* (1951).

Savage Sam

OLD YELLER'S son in Fred Gipson's novel *Savage Sam* (1962).

Scarlett

The heroine of Margaret Mitchell's *Gone With the Wind* (1936).

Schuster

See SIMON.

Selima

Horace Walpole's tabby cat who was immortalized in a poem by Thomas Gray. Selima drowned in a goldfish bowl while trying to catch a fish. (Indeed, "curiosity killed the cat!")

Sergeant Murphy

The brown dog that is a motorcycle-riding police officer in Richard Scarry's picture books.

Shakespeare (William)

(1564–1616) The English playwright who is known as history's greatest dramatist and the best English-language poet.

Shep

Shep, a collie that took care of a flock of sheep in New York City's Central Park, is described in an early twentieth-century story.

Shimbleshanks

One of the cats in *Old Possum's Book of Practical Cats* by T. S. Eliot (1939).

Simon

Co-founder of Simon & SCHUSTER, a major New York publisher.

Simpkin

The tailor's cat in Beatrix Potter's *The Tailor of Gloucester* (1903).

Sinbad (the Sailor)

The sailor whose adventures include battling monsters in *The Arabian Nights*.

SHAKESPEAREAN CHARACTERS	
Adonis	Juliet
Antony	Lysander
Ariel	Macbeth
Caesar	Othello
Hamlet	Puck
Horatio	Romeo

Snape (Severus)
Potions teacher at Hogwarts and the Half-Blood Prince in the *Harry Potter* series.

Sneakers
A cat about whom Margaret Wise Brown wrote in her *Seven Stories About a Cat Named Sneakers*.

Sophocles
A Greek playwright who wrote about the myths.

Sounder
The sharecropper's faithful dog with the resonant voice in William H. Armstrong's *Sounder* (1969).

Sour Mash
One of Mark Twain's several feline pets.

Stumpy
The big brown dog in Beatrix Potter's *The Tale of Little Pig Robinson* (1930).

Susie Salmon
Main character in the book *The Lovely Bones*.

Sweetheart
A dog referred to in Act 3, Scene 6 of SHAKESPEARE'S *King Lear* (1608).

Tabitha (Tabby)
A Siamese cat in *One Kitten Too Many* by Bianco Bradbury. Tabitha was called Tabby for short.

Tabitha Twitchit
The mother cat that was a shrewd businesswoman in Beatrix Potter's books.

Tailspin
The cat that was born on the moon in *Space Cat* by Ruthven Todd.

Tao
The male Siamese cat in *The Incredible Journey* (1961) by Sheila Burnford.

Tara
The O'Hara family's plantation in Margaret Mitchell's classic novel, *Gone With the Wind* (1936).

Tessa
A dog that belonged to author James Thurber.

Theocritus
An Alexandrian pastoral poet who wrote of the gods.

Tiger
The cat that played with KEEPER, the dog, in the household of Emily and Charlotte Brontë. (See also TIGER in Chapter 5.)

Tigger

The bouncy tiger in A. A. Milne's *The House at Pooh Corner* (1928).

Tinkerbell

The tiny fairy in *Peter Pan* (1904) by J. M. Barrie.

Titian

One of the greatest painters of the Renaissance. This Italian master lived c. 1488–1576.

Toby

(1) A puppet dog in the Punch and Judy shows. (2) The ugly part spaniel who assists Sherlock Holmes and Dr. Watson in Sir Arthur Conan Doyle's *The Sign of Four* (1890).

Tolkien, J.R.R.

Author of *The Lord of the Rings* and *The Hobbit*.

Tom Kitten

The naughty kitten in Beatrix Potter's *The Tale of Tom Kitten*, who was so fat his buttons burst off his clothes. He later lost his clothes, which were found by some ducks who wore them.

Tom Quartz

A kitten that President Theodore Roosevelt named for the fictional cat Tom Quartz in Mark Twain's book *Roughing It* (1872).

Toto

The dog who journeys with Dorothy in L. Frank Baum's *The Wonderful Wizard of Oz* (1900).

Toulouse-Lautrec (Henri de)

A leading Postimpressionist artist whose works depicted the sordid late nineteenth-century Parisian society.

Tray

The dog in Thomas Campbell's poem "The Harper."

Van Gogh (Vincent)

The Dutch Postimpressionist painter (1853–1890) whose works convey a wide spectrum of emotions.

Venus

Title character in the Shakespearean play *Venus and Adonis*.

Virgil

A Roman poet who wrote of the myths.

Volturri

The Vampire High Council in Stephenie Meyer's *Twilight* Saga.

Wilbur

The pig in *Charlotte's Web* by E. B. White.

William

(1) Charles Dickens's (1812–1870) dear white cat, which he renamed Williamina when she had kittens. (2) The egotistical cat obsessed with his own name in James Thurber's "The Cat in the Lifeboat" from *Further Fables for Our Time* (1956).

Winnie-the-Pooh

The opinionated but delightful hero of A. A. Milne's stories about a teddy bear and his friends.

Wolf

The dog that accompanied Rip Van Winkle on the day that he fell asleep for twenty years (from Washington Irving's story of Rip Van Winkle).

Zoroaster

One of Mark Twain's several cats.

11

Screen and Television

Who's the star of your household? Perhaps it's "Tonto," "Dracula," "Lassie," or maybe "Morris." Take your pick. But be careful; sometimes animals assume the characteristics of their namesakes. (Beware of "Pepe Le Pew.")

How About . . .

Angelina Jolie

Baloo

Batman

Bumblebee

Han Solo

Indiana Jones

Optimus Prime

Pluto

Rambo

Robin Sparkles

Spiderman

Tootsie

FAMOUS FICTIONAL ANIMALS

Apollo
One of the two doberman pinschers owned by Robbin Masters on the television series *Magnum P.I.* (See ZEUS.)

Arnold
The pet pig in the television series *Green Acres* starring Eddie Albert and Eva Gabor.

Asta
The wirehaired fox terrier in the television series *The Thin Man*. The Humane Association gave Asta two Patsy Awards for exceptional performance.

Babe
Title character in the movie *Babe*.

Benji
The shaggy mutt who became a star, appearing in *Benji* (1974), *For the Love of Benji* (1977), and *Oh Heavenly Dog* (1980).

Butkus
ROCKY'S dog in the original movie *Rocky*.

Charlie
The lead character in the animated movie *All Dogs Go To Heaven* (1989).

Cheshire Cat
The grinning cat who fades away except for his grin. Created by Lewis Carroll, the Cheshire Cat appeared in Walt Disney's animated movie *Alice in Wonderland* (1951). (See also CHESHIRE CAT in Chapter 10.)

Eddie
The dog who is Martin Crane's constant companion on *Frasier*.

Higgins
The dog in the television series *Petticoat Junction* (1963–1970). This was movie star BENJI'S first acting role.

Hooch
The large, ugly dog in the movie *Turner and Hooch* (1989).

"Cheshire Cat"

Kit

The name of the cat in the television series *Charmed*.

King Kong

Title character of the famous movie about an enormous gorilla who is captured in the wild and brought to New York City (1933, 2007).

Marley

Title character, a yellow Labrador Retriever, in the movie *Marley & Me*.

Morris

The famous cat that appeared in commercials for 9-Lives Cat Food. Morris also appeared in the movie *Shamus* (1973), and received the first Patsy Award for an animal in commercials.

Neil

The alcoholic St. Bernard from the television series *Topper*.

Old Yeller

The rugged, stray yellow-gold dog who was adopted in the movie *Old Yeller*, based on Fred Gipson's book *Old Yeller*. (See also OLD YELLER in Chapter 10.)

Rags

Carter's dog in the television series *Spin City*.

Rhubarb

The striped cat who played the lead role in the 1951 movie version of H. Allen Smith's *Rhubarb* (1946). Rhubarb won a Patsy Award for his performance, and then played Minerva in television's *Our Miss Brooks*. In 1962, Rhubarb won another Patsy as Cat in *Breakfast at Tiffany's*.

Rin Tin Tin

The German shepherd who after his first film, *Where the North Begins* (1923), appeared in more than forty movies in nine years. His offspring, all given the same name, appeared in subsequent movies and in the television series, *The Adventures of Rin Tin Tin*.

Scraps

The white mongrel with a brown spot over one eye, who costarred with CHARLIE CHAPLIN in *A Dog's Life* (1918). Scraps went on to star in fifty more films.

Solo

The puniest female pup in an African wild dog pack in Hugo van Lawick's television film *The Wild Dogs of Africa*.

Spuds Mackenzie

The bull terrier, who was known as the "Party Animal," and advertised Budweiser beer in television commercials.

Strongheart

The German shepherd who was the first canine hero of feature films.

Sugar Pie

The name of Anna Nicole Smith's dog from the television series *The Anna Nicole Show*.

Wishbone

A small dog who is the title character of the children's television series *Wishbone*.

Yukon King

The husky who aided Sergeant Preston of the Northwest Mounted Police in his television show, *Sergeant Preston of the Yukon*.

Zeus

One of the two Doberman pinschers owned by Robin Masters on the television series *Magnum P.I.* (See APOLLO.)

ACTORS YOU DON'T WANT TO MESS WITH

Brando (Marlon)

One of the most famous American actors after World War II. Brando won Academy Awards for his performances in *On the Waterfront* (1954) and *The Godfather* (1972).

Clint Eastwood

Academy Award winning actor, famous for his role in the Dirty Harry films.

De Niro (Robert)

Academy Award winner, Best Actor, for his role in the movie, *Raging Bull* (1980).

Ford (Harrison)

The actor who played Hans Solo in the *Star Wars* movie series. He also played Indiana Jones in *Raiders of the Lost Ark* and its sequels.

Hopkins (Anthony)

Academy Award winner, Best Actor, for his role in the movie, *The Silence of the Lambs* (1991).

John Wayne

The famous actor (1907–1979) best known for his portrayals of tough American Western Frontier characters and war heroes. He won an Academy Award in 1969 for *True Grit*.

Nicholson (Jack)

Academy Award winner, Best Actor, for his role in the movie, *One Flew Over the Cuckoo's Nest* (1975).

Pacino (Al)

Academy Award winner, Best Actor, for his role in the movie, *Scent of a Woman* (1992).

POPULAR FICTIONAL HEROES

Batman

Batman first appeared in *Detective Comics* in May 1939. In the spring of 1940, *Batman Comics* evolved. The Mutual Radio Network also featured the voices of Batman and ROBIN during the 1940s. The ABC television series ran from 1966 until 1968. The first movie *Batman* (1989) featured Michael Keaton in the title role. The second movie, *Batman Returns* (1992), also starred Michael Keaton. The third movie, *Batman Forever* (1995), starred Val Kilmer. The franchise was relaunched in 2005 starring actor Christian Bale as the masked crusader.

Buffy Summers

Main character in the TV series *Buffy the Vampire Slayer*.

Clarice Starling

FBI Agent sent to speak with convicted cannibal Hannibal Lector to uncover a serial killer in *Silence of the Lambs* (1990).

Ellen Ripley

Main protagonist in the *Alien* film franchise.

Forrest Gump

The title character in the Academy Award winning-movie starring TOM HANKS.

Han Solo

The courageous and snarky captain of the Millenium Falcon in the *Star Wars* films.

Indiana Jones

The swashbuckling hero of *Raiders of the Lost Ark* (and a series of movies that followed in the 1980s and in 2008), starring HARRISON FORD.

Jack Sparrow

The unpredictable main character in Disney's *The Pirates of the Caribbean* franchise. Played by Johnny Depp.

James T. Kirk

Captain of the Starship Enterprise in the original *Star Trek*.

John Connor

Leader of the future rebellion against the machines in the *Terminator* film franchise.

Lone Ranger

The masked hero of the television series *The Lone Ranger*.

Luke Skywalker

The hero of the movie *Stars Wars* (1977) and its sequels.

Morpheus

Neo's teacher and friend in *The Matrix* (1999) and its sequels.

Neo
The main character in *The Matrix* (1999) and its sequels.

007
The code number for the British spy James Bond, the hero of a series of movies based on novels by Ian Fleming.

Obi-Wan Kenobi
Jedi Master, teacher of Luke Skywalker and Darth Vader in the *Star Wars* film franchise.

Optimus Prime
Leader of the Autobots in the *Transformers* film franchise and cartoons.

Robin Hood
The rebellious leader of a group of men who stole from the rich and gave to the poor in England during the Crusades. Featured in many different TV shows and movies over the years.

Rocky Balboa
The boxer played by Sylvester Stallone in the *Rocky* movies.

Shrek
The grumpy ogre and title character in the Dreamworks film series *Shrek*.

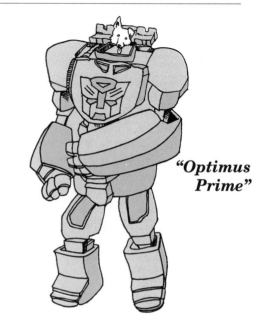

"Optimus Prime"

Spiderman
The masked superhero who has spider-like abilities.

Spock
The half Vulcan, half human first officer on the Starship *Enterprise* in the television series *Star Trek*.

Wolverine
One of the X-Men, who has super-accelerated healing powers and metal claws that come out of his knuckles. He is played by Hugh Jackman in the film franchise.

"Spock"

Yoda

LUKE SKYWALKER'S mentor who trains Luke to become a JEDI in the movies *The Empire Strikes Back* and *Return of the Jedi*.

DISNEY CHARACTERS

Aladdin

The diamond in the rough main character of Disney's *Aladdin* (1992).

Anita Campbell-Green-Dearly

Character in the animated movie *101 Dalmatians*.

Bagheera

The black panther in the Walt Disney movie *The Jungle Book* (1966).

Baloo

The bear in Walt Disney's movie *The Jungle Book* (1966).

Bambi

The fawn in Walt Disney's animated movie *Bambi* (1942).

Bashful

One of the Seven Dwarfs in the Walt Disney movie *Snow White and the Seven Dwarfs* (1937).

Belle

Main character in Disney's *Beauty and the Beast* (1991).

Buzz Lightyear

One of the main characters from the popular Disney film *Toy Story*.

Cinderella

The fairy-tale heroine who marries Prince Charming in Walt Disney's animated movie *Cinderella*.

Cruella de Vil

The villain in the animated movie *101 Dalmatians*.

Doc

One of the Seven Dwarfs in Walt Disney's animated movie *Snow White and the Seven Dwarfs* (1937).

Dopey

One of the Seven Dwarfs in Walt Disney's animated movie *Snow White and the Seven Dwarfs* (1937).

Dory

Character in the animated movie *Finding Nemo*.

Duchess

A Parisian cat in Walt Disney's animated movie, *The Aristocats* (1970). Duchess has a romance with O'Malley, the alley cat.

Dumbo

The title character and flying elephant in *Dumbo* (1941).

Eve

A robot sent back to Earth to locate plant life in *Wall-E* (2008).

Figaro

The kitten who kissed a fish in Walt Disney's animated film, *Pinocchio* (1940).

Flower

The skunk in the animated feature movie *Bambi* (1942).

Goofy

The not-so-bright, black hound who first appeared in Walt Disney's animated MICKEY MOUSE cartoons.

Grumpy

One of the Seven Dwarfs in Walt Disney's animated movie *Snow White and the Seven Dwarfs* (1937).

Happy

One of the Seven Dwarfs in Walt Disney's animated movie *Snow White and the Seven Dwarfs* (1937).

Horace

Character in the animated movie *101 Dalmatians*.

Jasper

Character in the animated movie *101 Dalmatians*.

Lady

The pretty female cocker spaniel who charmed TRAMP, a disreputable mutt, in Walt Disney Productions' *Lady and the Tramp*.

Malin

Character in the animated film *Finding Nemo*.

Mickey Mouse

The world famous star of numerous Walt Disney animated cartoons and movies, and of *The Mickey Mouse Club* television show.

Minnie Mouse

Animated cartoon star; MICKEY MOUSE'S female counterpart.

Mufasa

Simba's father and king of Pride Rock, a lion in the Walt Disney animated movie *The Lion King*.

Nala

Lioness and Simba's wife in the Walt Disney animated movie *The Lion King*.

Nanny

Character in the animated movie *101 Dalmatians*.

Nemo

Title character in the Disney film *Finding Nemo*.

Percy

The dog in Disney's animated movie *Pocahontas*.

Pluto

Walt Disney's lovable animated hound who appears with MICKEY MOUSE in many of his cartoons.

Pocahontas

Title character in Disney's 1995 animated movie about the Native American Indian maiden who fell in love with Captain John Smith.

Pumbaa

A warthog who befriends Simba in *The Lion King*.

Rafiki

The wise baboon in the Walt Disney animated movie *The Lion King*.

Roger Dearly Skinner

Character in the animated movie *101 Dalmatians*.

Scar

Uncle and foe of Simba in the animated movie *The Lion King*.

Simba

The lead character in the 1994 Walt Disney animated movie *The Lion King*.

Sleepy

One of the Seven Dwarfs in Walt Disney's animated movie *Snow White and the Seven Dwarfs* (1937).

Sneezy

One of the Seven Dwarfs in Walt Disney's animated movie *Snow White and the Seven Dwarfs* (1937).

Snow White

The fairy tale heroine of Walt Disney's animated movie *Snow White and the Seven Dwarfs* (1937).

Thumper

The rabbit in Walt Disney's animated movie *Bambi* (1942). (See BAMBI.)

Timon

Befriends Simba in the Walt Disney animated movie *The Lion King*.

Tinkerbell

The tiny fairy in the Walt Disney movie *Peter Pan*.

Tramp

The stray dog who fell in love with LADY, the pretty cocker spaniel, in Walt Disney Productions' animated feature *Lady and the Tramp*.

Wall-E

The title robotic character from the Disney movie *Wall-E*.

Woody

Main character of the Disney film *Toy Story*.

Zazu

One of Scar's Hyena companions in the Walt Disney animated movie *The Lion King*.

BEVERLY HILLS CHIHUAHUAS	
Chico	El Diablo
Chloe	Manuel
Chucho	Monte
Delgado	Papi
Delta	Rafa

MORE SCREEN AND TELEVISION NAMES

Abbott (Bud)

The sly con man in the Abbott and COSTELLO comedy team of the 1930s, '40s, and '50s.

Adrien Brody

Academy Award Winner, Best Actor, for his role in the Pianist (2003).

Al

TIM'S "assistant" in the 1999s television series *Home Improvement*.

Alfred

Bruce Wayne's faithful butler in the *Batman* franchise.

Alice Kramden

The wife of RALPH KRAMDEN, played by JACKIE GLEASON, in the 1950s television series *The Honeymooners*.

Angel

Vampire with a soul, character on *Buffy the Vampire Slayer* and title character in the spin-off *Angel*.

Angelina Jolie

Academy Award winner, Best Supporting Actress, for her role in the movie *Girl, Interrupted* (1999).

Anna Magnani

Academy Award winner, Best Actress, for her role in the movie, *The Rose Tattoo* (1955).

Anne Bancroft

Academy Award winner, Best Actress, for her role in the movie, *The Miracle Worker* (1962).

Archie Bunker

The bigoted character played by Carroll O'Connor in the television series *All in the Family*.

Art Carney

Academy Award winner, Best Actor, for his role in the movie, *Harry and Tonto* (1974). Friend of RALPH KRAMDEN, played by JACKIE GLEASON, in the 1950s television series *The Honeymooners*.

Arthur Hoggett

Character in the movie *Babe*.

Audrey Hepburn

Academy Award winner, Best Actress, for her role in the movie, *Roman Holiday* (1953).

B. J. Hunnicut

HAWKEYE'S buddy on the television series *M*A*S*H*.

Bailey

A character in the television series *Party of Five*.

Barbra Streisand

Academy Award winner, Best Actress, for her role in the movie *Funny Girl* (1968).

AND THE OSCAR GOES TO . . .	
Adrien Brody	DiCaprio
Angelina Jolie	Halle
Audrey Hepburn	Kate Winslet
Barbra Streisand	Marion Cotillard
Ben Kingsley	Meryl Streep
Charlize	Nicole Kidman
Daniel Day-Lewis	Paul Newman
Denzel	

Barnabas Collins

The vampire in the television series *Dark Shadows*.

Barnaby Jones

The private eye played by Buddy Ebsen in the television series *Barnaby Jones*.

Barney Fife

The bungling deputy (1960–1965) in the television series *The Andy Griffith Show*.

Barney Stintson

Breakout character on the sitcom *How I Met Your Mother*, played by Neil Patrick Harris.

Bart Maverick

One of the brothers, played by Jack Kelly, living in the frontier west in the television series *Maverick*.

Beaver (Cleaver)

The hapless younger son of the Cleavers in the television series *Leave It to Beaver*.

Beeswax

A cat in the 1989 Tom Selleck film *Her Alibi*.

Ben Kingsley

Academy Award winner, Best Actor, for his role in the movie, *Gandhi* (1982).

Bert

One of the muppet characters in the television series *Sesame Street*. (See ERNIE and OSCAR THE GROUCH.)

Bette Davis

Academy Award winner, Best Actress, for her roles in the movies *Dangerous* (1935), and *Jezebel* (1938).

Bing Crosby

Academy Award winner, Best Actor, for his role in the movie, *Going My Way* (1944).

Blaire Waldorf

Queen B of the Upper East Side on the TV show *Gossip Girl*.

Bloop Bloop

The extraterrestrial creature from the television series *Lost in Space* (1965–1968).

Bojangles (Bill Robinson)

A dancer and entertainer (1878–1949), appeared in SHIRLEY TEMPLE movies.

Bones

Nickname of Temperance Brennan, a forensic anthropologist and title character of the popular TV show *Bones*.

Boo-Boo Kitty

SHIRLEY'S stuffed cat in the television series *Laverne and Shirley*.

Bosley

The man who acts as an intermediary between the elusive Charlie and his female detectives in the television series *Charlie's Angels*.

Brady

The name of the family in the television series *The Brady Bunch*.

Bree Hodge

One of main characters from the television series *Desperate Housewives*.

Bret Maverick

One of the brothers, played by James Garner, living in the frontier west in the television series *Maverick*.

Brewster

The baseball player, played by Richard Pryor, who inherits a fortune in the movie *Brewster's Millions*.

Broderick Crawford

Academy Award winner, Best Actor, for his role in the movie, *All the King's Men* (1949).

Brubaker

The prison inspector played by Robert Redford in the movie *Brubaker*.

Bubba

The friend of FORREST GUMP in the Academy Award-winning (1994) movie *Forrest Gump* starring TOM HANKS.

Buffy

The little blonde-haired girl in the television series *Family Affair*.

Bumblebee

An alien robot sent to protect Shia Lebouf's character, Sam Witwicky, in the *Transformers* film franchise.

Burt Lancaster

Academy Award winner, Best Actor, for his role in the movie, *Elmer Gantry* (1960).

Burt Reynolds

Actor who has starred in a variety of movies in the 1960s, '70s, and '80s.

Butch Cassidy

The western outlaw played by PAUL NEWMAN in the 1969 movie *Butch Cassidy and the Sundance Kid*. (See SUNDANCE KID.)

Car Face

The sinister gang leader "Junkyard Dog" in the 1989 animated cartoon *All Dogs Go to Heaven*.

Carrie Bradshaw

Columnist played by Sarah Jessica Parker on the television series *Sex and the City*.

Cat Ballou

The main character of the 1965 movie *Cat Ballou*.

Chandler Bing

Businessman played by Matthew Perry in the television series *Friends*.

Charlie Chaplin

One of the most famous actors in motion picture history. Chaplin is best remembered for his roles in silent films.

Charlize (Theron)

Academy Award Winner, Best Actress, for her role in *Monster* (2004).

Charlotte York

An art gallery curator played by Kristin Davis on *Sex and the City*.

Charlton Heston

Academy Award winner, Best Actor, for his role in the movie, *Ben Hur* (1959).

Cher

Best-selling singer and Academy Award winner, Best Actress, for her role in the movie, *Moonstruck* (1987).

"Chewbacca"

Chewbacca (or Chewy)

The 100-year-old "Wookie" in the movie *Star Wars* (1977) and its sequels.

Clarabell

The puppet clown in the 1950s television series *Howdy Doody*.

Clark Gable

The popular American film star (1901–1960) once called "The King," best known for his role as Rhett Butler in the 1939 movie *Gone With the Wind*.

Clark Griswold

The lead character in the National Lampoon *Vacation* movie series starring Chevy Chase.

Claudette Colbert

Academy Award winner, Best Actress, for her role in the movie, *It Happened One Night* (1934).

Cliff Robertson

Academy Award winner, Best Actor, for his role in the movie, *Charly* (1968).

Costello (Lou)

The rotund victimized member of the ABBOTT and Costello comedy team.

Cuba Gooding, Jr.

Academy Award winner, Best Supporting Actor, for his role in the movie *Jerry Maguire*.

Daniel Day-Lewis

Two-time Academy Award winner, Best Actor, for his role in the movies, *My Left Foot* (1989) and *There Will Be Blood* (2008).

Daphne Moon

Former housekeeper played by Jane Leeves on the television series *Frasier*.

Darth Vader

The main antagonist in the movie *Star Wars* (1977) and its sequels.

Denzel (Washington)

Academy Award Winner, Best Actor, for his role in *Training Day* (2002).

Dexter

Title character on the TV series *Dexter*.

Diane Keaton

Academy Award winner, Best Actress, for her role in the movie, *Annie Hall* (1977).

DiCaprio (Leonardo)

Actor most famous for his roles in the movies *William Shakespeare's Romeo & Juliet, Titanic*, and *The Departed*, among others.

Dobie Gillis

A romantically inclined teenage boy in the television series *The Many Loves of Dobie Gillis*. Dobie also appeared in the movie *The Affairs of Dobie Gillis* (1953).

Dolly (Parton)

The country western singer, song writer, and actress (*Nine to Five*). She appeared in her own television variety show *Dolly*. She also opened her own theme park, Dollywood, in Tennessee in 1986.

Dracula

The vampire created by the novelist Bram Stoker, who first appeared in the 1931 movie *Dracula, The Un-Dead*. Based on the historical figure "Vlad the Impaler."

Dudley (Moore)

The contemporary comedian and movie star. A popular British comedian and actor.

Duke

An airedale owned by famous Western actor John Wayne. The dog's name inspired Wayne's nickname, "The Duke."

Dustin Hoffman

Academy Award winner, Best Actor, for his roles in the movies, *Kramer vs. Kramer* (1979), and *Rain Man* (1988).

Echo

Code name of the main character on the popular TV show *Dollhouse*.

E. T.

The extraterrestrial being in Steven Spielberg's movie *E.T.*

Elaine

A character on the television series *Seinfeld* played by Julia Louis-Dreyfus.

Elizabeth Taylor

Academy Award winner, Best Actress, for her roles in the movies, *Butterfield 8* (1960), and *Who's Afraid of Virginia Woolf?* (1965).

Elsa

The lioness whose story is told in the movie *Born Free* and in a television series. Elsa's story was first told in a book by Joy Adamson.

Ernest Borgnine

Academy Award winner, Best Actor, for his role in the movie, *Marty* (1954).

Ernie

One of the muppet characters in the television series *Sesame Street*. (See BERT and OSCAR THE GROUCH.)

Esmé Hoggett

Character in the movie *Babe*.

Ethel Mertz

The wife of Fred Mertz in the *I Love Lucy* television series.

Ewok

A race of furry, teddy-bearlike creatures featured in the movie *The Return of the Jedi*.

F. Murray Abraham

Academy Award winner, Best Actor, for his role in the movie, *Amadeus* (1984).

Fantasia

A 1940 Walt Disney feature film that redefined cinema.

Farrah (Fawcett)

An actress who first became famous in the television series *Charlie's Angels*.

Faye Dunaway

Academy Award winner, Best Actress, for her role in the movie, *Network* (1976).

Felix

The fussy character played by Jack Lemmon in the movie *The Odd Couple* and by Tony Randall in the television series.

Ferdinand

Character in the movie *Babe*.

Festus

The old deputy in the television series *Gunsmoke*.

Fez

Foreign exchange student played by Wilmer Valderrama on the television series *That 70's Show*.

Fly

Character in the movie *Babe*.

Fonzie

The nickname of the cool high school dropout, played by Henry Winkler, in the television series *Happy Days*.

Forest (Whitaker)

Academy Award Winner, Best Actor, for his role in *The Last King of Scotland* (2007).

Frances McDormand

Academy Award winner, Best Actress, for her role in the movie *Fargo* (1996).

Frank Sinatra

Academy Award winner, Best Supporting Actor, for his role in the movie, *From Here to Eternity* (1953).

Frasier Crane

Psychologist and radio host played by Kelsey Grammer on the television series *Frasier*.

Fredric March

Academy Award winner, Best Actor, for his roles in the movies, *Dr. Jekyll and Mr. Hyde* (1932), and *The Best Years of Our Lives* (1946).

Frodo Baggins

A hobbit played by Elijah Wood in the movie trilogy *The Lord of the Rings*.

Screen and Television

Gary Cooper

Academy Award winner, Best Actor, for his roles in the movies, *Sergeant York* (1941), and *High Noon* (1952).

Gene Hackman

Academy Award winner, Best Actor, for his role in the movie, *The French Connection* (1971).

Geoffrey Rush

Academy Award winner, Best Actor, for his role in the movie *Shine* (1996).

George

Jerry's neurotic friend in the television series *Seinfeld* played by Jason Alexander.

George Arliss

Academy Award winner, Best Actor, for his role in the movie, *Disraeli* (1930).

George Banks

The lead character played by Steve Martin in the movie *Father of the Bride*.

George Carlin

Popular comedian whose stand ups and shows were often banned because of controversy.

George C. Scott

Academy Award winner, Best Actor, for his role in the movie, *Patton* (1970).

Geraldine Page

Academy Award winner, Best Actress, for her role in the movie, *The Trip to Bountiful* (1985).

Giles (Rupert)

Librarian, trainer, and father figure to Buffy in *Buffy the Vampire Slayer*.

Glenda Jackson

Academy Award winner, Best Actress, for her roles in the movies, *Women in Love* (1970), and *A Touch of Class* (1973).

Glenn Close

Winner of the Tony Award for Best Leading Actress in the musical *Sunset Boulevard*; well-known screen star (*Fatal Attraction, The Big Chill*).

Goose

The call sign of a pilot in the movie *Top Gun*.

Gordon Gecco

The character played by MICHAEL DOUGLAS in the movie *Wall Street*.

Grace Kelly

Academy Award winner, Best Actress, for her role in the movie, *The Country Girl* (1954).

Greer Garson

Academy Award winner, Best Actress, for the movie, *Mrs. Miniver* (1942).

Gregory Peck

Academy Award winner, Best Actor, for his role in the movie, *To Kill a Mockingbird* (1962).

Grunt

The dog in the movie *Flashdance*.

Gwyneth Paltrow

Academy Award winner, Best Actress, for her role in the movie *Shakespeare in Love* (1998).

Halle (Berry)

Academy Award Winner, Best Actress, for her role in *Monster's Ball* (2002).

Hardy (Oliver)

The comedian who co-starred with his partner, LAUREL, in numerous movies.

Harriet (Hilliard Nelson)

The wife of OZZIE in the television series *The Adventures of Ozzie and Harriet* (1952–1966).

Hawkeye

The irreverent doctor played by Alan Alda in the classic television series *M*A*S*H*.

Hazel (Burke)

The family maid played by Shirley Booth in the television series *Hazel*.

Helen Hunt

Academy Award winner, Best Actress, for her role in the movie *As Good As It Gets* (1997).

Helen Mirren

Academy Award Winner, Best Actress, for her role in the movie *The Queen* (2006).

Henry Fonda

Academy Award winner, Best Actor, for his role in the movie, *On Golden Pond* (1981).

Herbie

"The Love Bug," a Volkswagen, who is the hero in several movies.

Hilary Swank

Two-time Academy Award winner, Best Actress, for her role in the movie *Boys Don't Cry* (1999) and *Million Dollar Baby* (2005).

Holly Hunter

Academy Award winner, Best Actress, for her role in the movie, *The Piano* (1993).

House (Greg)

The title character of the medical drama *House*.

Humphrey Bogart

Academy Award winner, Best Actor, for his role in the movie, *The African Queen* (1951).

Ice Man

The call sign of a pilot played by Val Kilmer in the movie *Top Gun*.

Igor

Dr. Frankenstein's assistant in a series of movies about Frankenstein's monster.

Ingrid Bergman

Academy Award winner, Best Actress, for her roles in the movies, *Gaslight* (1944), and *Anastasia* (1956).

J.D.

Main character on the TV show *Scrubs*.

J. R. (Ewing)

The ruthless Texas oilman in the television series *Dallas*.

Jack Lemmon

Academy Award winner, Best Actor, for his role in the movie, *Save the Tiger* (1973).

Jackie Gleason

Actor and entertainer best known for his role as RALPH KRAMDEN in the 1950s television series *The Honeymooners*.

James Cagney

Academy Award winner, Best Actor, for his role in the movie, *Yankee Doodle Dandy* (1942).

James Stewart

Academy Award winner, Best Actor, for his role in the movie, *The Philadelphia Story* (1940).

Jamie Foxx

Academy Award Winner, Best Actor, for his role in *Ray* (2005).

Jane Fonda

Academy Award winner, Best Actress, for her roles in the movies, *Klute* (1971), and *Coming Home* (1978).

Jane Wyman

Academy Award winner, Best Actress, for her role in the movie, *Johnny Belinda* (1948).

Janet Gaynor

Academy Award winner, Best Actress, for her role in the movie, *Seventh Heaven* (1927).

Jay Leno

Former host of *The Tonight Show*.

Jeremy Irons

Academy Award winner, Best Actor, for his role in the movie, *Reversal of Fortune* (1990). Was the voice of Scar in the beloved Disney film *The Lion King*.

Jerry

The famous mouse who, with his partner, the cat TOM, has appeared in numerous MGM, and later Hanna-Barbera, animated cartoons.

Jessica Lange

Academy Award winner, Best Actress, for her role in the movie, *Blue Sky* (1994).

Jessica Tandy

Academy Award winner, Best Actress, for her role in the movie, *Driving Miss Daisy* (1989).

Jessica

The part played by Angela Lansbury in the popular, long-running television series *Murder She Wrote*.

Joan Crawford

Academy Award winner, Best Actress, for her role in the movie, *Mildred Pierce* (1945).

Joan Fontaine

Academy Award winner, Best Actress, for her role in the movie, *Suspicion* (1941).

Joanne Woodward

Academy Award winner, Best Actress, for her role in the movie, *The Three Faces of Eve* (1957).

Jodie Foster

Academy Award winner, Best Actress, for her roles in the movies, *The Accused* (1988), and *The Silence of the Lambs* (1991).

Joey Tribbiani

Struggling actor played by Matt LeBlanc on *Friends*.

John Becker

Physician played by Ted Danson on the television series *Becker*.

John Locke

One of the main characters on the popular TV show *Lost*.

Jon Voight

Academy Award winner, Best Actor, for his role in the movie, *Coming Home* (1978).

Joker

The sinister character of *Batman* fame played by Heath Ledger in *The Dark Knight*. Also played by Cesar Romero in the television series and by Jack Nicholson in the 1989 movie. (See BATMAN.)

Jose Ferrer

Academy Award winner, Best Actor, for his role in the movie, *Cyrano de Bergerac* (1950).

Screen and Television

Julia Roberts

Academy Award Winner, Best Actress, for her role in *Erin Brockovich* (2001).

Julie Andrews

Academy Award winner, Best Actress, for her role in the movie, *Mary Poppins* (1964). Also starred in *The Sound of Music*.

Julie Christie

Academy Award winner, Best Actress, for her role in the movie, *Darling* (1965).

MEMORABLE CHARACTERS	
Archie Bunker	Fonzie
Barnabas Collins	House
Barney Stintson	Kramer
Blaire Waldorf	Lucy Ricardo
Bree Hodge	MacGyver
Carrie Bradshaw	Rocky Balboa
Dexter	Veronica Mars
Echo	

Kate Winslet

Academy Award Winner, Best Actress, for her role in *The Reader* (2008).

Katharine Hepburn

Academy Award winner, Best Actress, for her roles in the movies, *Morning Glory* (1932), *Guess Who's Coming to Dinner?* (1967), *The Lion in Winter* (1968), and *On Golden Pond* (1981).

Kathie Lee

Former co-host of the television talk show *Regis and Kathie Lee*.

Kathy Bates

Academy Award winner, Best Actress, for her role in the movie, *Misery* (1990).

Kevin Spacey

Academy Award winner, Best Actor, for his role in the movie, *American Beauty* (1999).

Kiara

Lioness in the Walt Disney animated movie *The Lion King: Simba's Pride*.

Kimba

The lead character in the 1960s Japanese created television cartoon *Kimba, the White Lion*.

Kingfish

George Stevens's title on the television series *Amos 'n Andy*.

Kramer

Jerry's eccentric next-door neighbor in the television series *Seinfeld* played by Michael Richards.

Kunta Kinte

The African man captured by slave traders and shipped to America in the television mini-series *Roots* (1977).

Larry

One of the characters in the movie series *The Three Stooges*.

Lassie

The collie heroine of the movie *Lassie Come Home* (1943), based on a novel by Eric Knight. This Lassie, followed by many generations of descendants, starred in seven movie sequels, "The Lassie Radio Show," and the *Lassie* television series.

Laurel (Stan)

The slapstick comedian who co-starred with his partner, HARDY, in numerous movies.

Laurence Olivier

Academy Award winner, Best Actor, for his role in the movie, *Hamlet* (1948).

Laverne

Title character, played by Penny Marshall, in the 1970s television series *Laverne and Shirley*.

Lee Marvin

Academy Award winner, Best Actor, for his role in the movie, *Cat Ballou* (1965).

Leo

The Metro-Goldwyn-Mayer (MGM) trademark—a lion that appeared on screen in hundreds of movies.

Little Orphan Annie

The little girl created in a comic strip of the same name by Harold Gray in 1924. Little Orphan Annie has appeared in several movies, the first in 1932.

Liza Minnelli

Academy Award winner, Best Actress, for her role in the movie, *Cabaret* (1972).

Loretta Young

Academy Award winner, Best Actress, for her role in the movie, *The Farmer's Daughter* (1947).

Louise Fletcher

Academy Award winner, Best Actress, for her role in the movie, *One Flew Over the Cuckoo's Nest* (1975).

Lucy Ricardo

RICKY RICARDO'S wife and star of the 1950s *I Love Lucy* television series starring Lucille Ball.

Maa

Character in the movie *Babe*.

MacGyver

The title character of a television series.

Maggie Smith

Academy Award winner, Best Actress, for her role in the movie, *The Prime of Miss Jean Brodie* (1969).

Magnum (Thomas)

The private investigator played by Tom Selleck in the television series *Magnum, P.I.*

Marilyn Monroe

Famous celebrity and personality known for her blonde hair and voluptuousness.

Marion Cotillard

Academy Award Winner, Best Actress, for her role in *La Vie en Rose* (2007).

Mary Pickford

Academy Award winner, Best Actress, for her role in the movie, *Coquette* (1928).

Matt Groening

Creator of *The Simpsons* and *Futurama*.

Maverick

The pilot call sign of the lead character played by Tom Cruise in the movie *Top Gun*. Also title of a television series starring James Garner.

Maximilian Schell

Academy Award winner, Best Actor, for his role in the movie, *Judgment at Nuremberg* (1961).

Maynard (G. Krebs)

DOBIE GILLIS'S beatnik buddy in the television series *The Many Loves of Dobie Gillis*.

McCloud

The cowboy detective in the television series *McCloud*.

McDreamy

Nickname for one of the main characters, Dr. Derek Shepherd, on *Grey's Anatomy*.

McLovin

One of the main characters in the 2008 comedy *Superbad*.

Meatball

A mixed-breed dog who appeared in *Black Sheep Squadron*, a television series with Robert Conrad.

Meathead

ARCHIE BUNKER'S derogatory name for his son-in-law in the television series *All in the Family*.

Megatron

Villainous leader of the Decepticons, enemies of the Autobots in *Transformers*.

Mel Gibson

Actor and star of numerous movies including *Mad Max*, the *Lethal Weapon* series, and *Braveheart*, which he also directed.

Meryl Streep

Academy Award winner, Best Actress, for her role in the movie, *Sophie's Choice* (1982).

Mia (Farrow)

An actress who has appeared in a variety of movies, including several by Woody Allen.

Michael Douglas

Academy Award winner, Best Actor, for his role in the movie, *Wall Street* (1987).

Mickey Rooney

The movie actor known for his movies with Judy Garland in the 1930s and '40s, his Andy Hardy movies, and his part in *National Velvet* (1944).

Mike Judge

Creator of the television series *Beavis and Butthead* and the television series *King of the Hill*.

Milo

Title character in the movie *Milo and Otis*.

Miranda Hobbes

Lawyer played by Cynthia Nixon on *Sex and the City*.

Miss Ellie

J. R. EWING'S mother in the television series *Dallas*.

Miss Kitty

The owner of Dodge City's bar in the television series *Gunsmoke*.

Miss Piggy

The outrageous leading lady of television's *The Muppet Show* and of *The Muppet Movie* (1979).

Moe

One of the characters in *The Three Stooges*.

Monica Geller

Chef played by Courteney Cox on *Friends*.

Mr. T

The impressively large actor who appeared in the television series *The A-Team* and with SYLVESTER STALLONE in one of the sequels to the movie *Rocky*.

Munchkin

One of a group of little people visited by Dorothy in the cinema classic, *The Wizard of Oz*.

Navin

The character played by Steve Martin in the movie *The Jerk*.

Newman

Postman played by Wayne Knight on *Seinfeld*.

Nicole Kidman

Academy Award Winner, Best Actress, for her role in *The Hours* (2003).

Niles Crane, Dr.

Frasier's brother, played by David Hyde Pierce, on *Frasier*.

Nina Banks

Played by Diane Keaton, co-star and wife of character George Banks in the movie *Father of the Bride*.

Olivia de Havilland

Academy Award winner, Best Actress, for her roles in the movies, *To Each His Own* (1946), and *The Heiress* (1949).

Omar (Sharif)

A Middle Eastern actor who appeared in numerous movies.

Opie

The boy who portrayed the young son of Andy Griffith in the television series *The Andy Griffith Show*.

Oprah Winfrey

Television talk show hostess and personality.

Oscar

The sloppy character played by Walter Matthau in the movie *The Odd Couple* and by Jack Klugman in the television series.

Oscar the Grouch

One of the muppet characters in the television series *Sesame Street*. (See BERT and ERNIE.)

Otis

Title character in the movie *Milo and Otis*.

Otto

CHARLIE'S buddy in the 1989 musical cartoon *All Dogs Go to Heaven*.

Ozzie (Nelson)

Main character and husband of HARRIET on the television series *The Adventures of Ozzie and Harriet*.

Patricia Neal

Academy Award winner, Best Actress, for her role in the movie, *Hud* (1963).

Paul Newman

Academy Award winner, Best Actor, for his role in the movie, *The Color of Money* (1986).

Paul Scofield

Academy Award winner, Best Actor, for his role in the movie, *A Man for All Seasons* (1966).

Pegleg Pete

The villainous bulldog with a wooden leg who appeared with MICKEY MOUSE in the Walt Disney films, *Steamboat Willie* (1928) and *Gallopin' Gaucho* (1929).

Peter Pan

The principal character in a play by J. M. Barrie about a boy who didn't want to grow up. Subsequently, he was recreated in the Walt Disney animated movie *Peter Pan*.

Philip Seymour Hoffman

Academy Award Winner, Best Actor, for his role in *Capote* (2005).

Phoebe Buffay

Bubbly blonde played by Lisa Kudrow on *Friends*.

Popeye

The sailor who derives his strength from eating spinach. Popeye appeared first in comic strips, and later in animated cartoons and movies.

"Popeye"

Potsie

Richie Cunningham's friend in the television series *Happy Days*.

Princess Leia

The heroine of the movie *Stars Wars* (1977) and its sequels.

Pyewacket

The cat in the film *Bell, Book, and Candle*.

Quincy
Title character in the television series starring Jack Klugman who played a medical examiner.

Rachel Green
Prissy character played by Jennifer Aniston on *Friends*.

Radar
The bespectacled corporal with E.S.P. in the television series *M*A*S*H*.

Ralph Kramden
The high-strung bus driver played by JACKIE GLEASON in the television series *The Honeymooners*.

Rambo
The character played by SYLVESTER STALLONE in the movie *First Blood* and its sequels.

Ray Barone
Character played by Ray Romano in the television series *Everybody Loves Raymond*.

Ray Milland
Academy Award winner, Best Actor, for his role in the movie, *The Lost Weekend* (1945).

Reese Witherspoon
Academy Award Winner, Best Actress, for her role in *Walk the Line* (2005).

Rex
Character in the movie *Babe*.

Rex Harrison
Academy Award winner, Best Actor, for his role in the movie, *My Fair Lady* (1964).

Rhett Butler
A character played by Clark Gable in the movie *Gone With the Wind* (1939), based on the book by Margaret Mitchell.

Richard Dreyfuss
Academy Award winner, Best Actor, for his role in the movie, *The Goodbye Girl* (1977).

Ricky Ricardo
Lucy's husband and band leader played by Desi Arnaz in the popular television series *I Love Lucy*.

Robert Barone
Ray's brother, played by Brad Garrett, on *Everybody Loves Raymond*.

Robert Donat
Academy Award winner, Best Actor, for his role in the movie, *Goodbye Mr. Chips* (1939).

Robert Duvall

Academy Award winner, Best Actor, for his role in the movie, *Tender Mercies* (1983).

Roberto Benigni

Academy Award winner, Best Actor, for his role in the movie *Life Is Beautiful* (1998).

Robin

The younger half of the BATMAN and Robin combination known as "The Dynamic Duo."

Robin Sparkles

Alternate pop-music icon personality of Robin Scherbatsky, one of the main characters on the sitcom *How I Met Your Mother*.

Rochester (Van Jones)

Jack Benny's valet, played by Eddie Anderson.

Rockford

The private detective played by James Garner on the television series *The Rockford Files*.

Rocky Balboa

The boxer played by SYLVESTER STALLONE in the movie *Rocky* and its sequels.

Rod Steiger

Academy Award winner, Best Actor, for his role in the movie, *In the Heat of the Night* (1967).

Ronald Colman

Academy Award winner, Best Actor, for his role in the movie, *A Double Life* (1947).

Ross Geller

Paleontologist played by David Schwimmer on *Friends*.

Roz Doyle

The on-air radio producer played by Peri Gilpin on *Frasier*.

Russell Crowe

Academy Award winner, Best Actor, for his role in *Gladiator* (2000).

Sally Field

Academy Award winner, Best Actress, for her roles in the movies *Norma Rae* (1979), and *Places in the Heart* (1984).

Samantha Jones

Publicist played by Kim Cattrall on *Sex and the City*.

Sapphire

The wife of George "Kingfish" Stevens in the television series *Amos 'n Andy*. (See KINGFISH.)

Sawyer

One of the main characters in the TV show *Lost*.

Scarlett (O'Hara)

The heroine, played by Vivien Leigh, of the classic movie *Gone With the Wind* (1939), based on the book by Margaret Mitchell.

Sean Penn

Academy Award Winner, Best Actor, for his roles in *Mystic River* (2004), and *Milk* (2008).

Seeley Boothe

One of the main characters on the TV series *Bones*.

Seinfeld (Jerry)

Entertainer and star of the popular television series *Seinfeld*.

Sheena

The "Queen of the Jungle" played by Irish McCalla in both the movie and the television series.

Shirley

Title character played by Cindy Williams in the television series *Laverne and Shirley*.

Shirley Booth

Academy Award winner, Best Actress, for her role in the movie *Come Back Little Sheba* (1952).

Shirley MacLaine

Academy Award winner, Best Actress, for her role in the movie *Terms of Endearment* (1983).

Shirley Temple

The most popular child actress of the 1930s, best remembered for her dimples and blonde curly hair.

Shogun

The Japanese warrior in the television movie *Shogun*.

Sidney Poitier

Academy Award winner, Best Actor, for his role in the movie, *Lillies of the Field* (1963).

Sir Alec Guinness

Academy Award winner, Best Actor, for his role in the movie, *The Bridge Over the River Kwai* (1957). Played Obi-Wan Kenobi in the original *Star Wars* trilogy.

Sissy Spacek

Academy Award winner, Best Actress, for her role in the movie, *Coal Miner's Daughter* (1980).

Sly

The nickname for actor SYLVESTER STALLONE.

Sookie Stackhouse

Main character on the popular TV show *True Blood*.

Sophia Loren

Academy Award winner, Best Actress, for her role in the movie, *Two Women* (1961).

Spanky

The fat little boy in the television series *The Little Rascals*.

Spencer Tracy

Academy Award winner, Best Actor, for his roles in the movies, *Captains Courageous* (1937), and *Boys Town* (1938).

Squeaky

The little girl in the 1989 animated movie *All Dogs Go To Heaven*.

Striker

The call sign of a pilot in the movie *Top Gun*.

Sundance Kid

The western outlaw played by Robert Redford in the 1969 movie *Butch Cassidy and the Sundance Kid*. (See BUTCH CASSIDY.)

Superman

The man of steel. Played by Christopher Reeves in the original *Superman* movies, and by Tom Wellings in the TV series *Smallville*.

Susan Hayward

Academy Award winner, Best Actress, for her role in the movie, *I Want to Live* (1958).

Susan Sarandon

Academy Award winner, Best Actress, for her role in the movie *Dead Man Walking* (1995).

Sylar

The sometimes antagonist who kills other heroes on the TV show *Heroes*.

Sydney Bristow

The double agent main character of the TV show *Alias*. Played by Jennifer Garner.

Sylvester Stallone

The actor who has starred in the ROCKY movies and the RAMBO movies.

T. C.

THOMAS MAGNUM'S friend, who pilots a helicopter in the television series *Magnum, P.I.*

Tar Baby

The inanimate baby who mystified all the animals in the Walt Disney movie *Song of the South* (1946); based on Joel Chandler Harris's stories.

Ted Mosby

Main character on the sitcom *How I Met Your Mother*.

Terminator

Title character in a movie series starring Arnold Schwarzenegger.

Tigger

The bouncy tiger in the animated television versions of A. A. Milne's *Winnie-the-Pooh* stories.

Tim

The star of the television series *Home Improvement*.

Toby

KUNTA KINTE'S name as a slave in the television mini-series *Roots* (1977).

Tom Hanks

Academy Award winner, Best Actor, for his roles in the movies, *Philadelphia* (1993), and *Forrest Gump* (1994).

Tom

The famous cat who, with his partner, the mouse JERRY, has appeared in numerous MGM, and later Hanna-Barbera animated cartoons.

Tonto

The LONE RANGER'S Native American Indian companion in both the movie and the television series about *The Lone Ranger*.

Tootsie

The man-turned-woman, played by DUSTIN HOFFMAN in the movie *Tootsie*.

Toto

Dorothy's dog in the movie *The Wizard of Oz* (1939).

Trapper

HAWKEYE'S buddy in the television series *M*A*S*H*.

Veronica Mars

Title character of the noir TV show *Veronica Mars*.

Victor McLaglen

Academy Award winner, Best Actor, for his role in the movie, *The Informer* (1935).

Vivien Leigh

Academy Award winner, Best Actress, for her roles in the movies, *Gone With the Wind* (1939), and *A Streetcar Named Desire* (1951).

Wallace Beery

Academy Award winner, Best Actor, for his role in the movie, *The Champ* (1931).

Wally (Cleaver)

BEAVER'S older brother in the television series *Leave It to Beaver*.

Warner Baxter

Academy Award winner, Best Actor, for his role in the movie, *In Old Arizona* (1928).

William Hurt

Academy Award winner, Best Actor, for his role in the movie, *Kiss of the Spider Woman* (1985).

Wilson

TIM and JILL'S next door neighbor in the television series *Home Improvement*.

Wonder Woman

Title character of the superhero played by Lynda Carter in the 1970s television series based on the comic book heroine of the 1940s.

Xena

Title character of the television series *Xena, Warrior Princess*.

Yul Brynner

Academy Award winner, Best Actor, for his role in the movie, *The King and I* (1956).

12

Locations and Places

If you're caught without a map or GPS, check this chapter—you'll find that little spot you've been looking for. Or, pick your favorite place in the world as your pet's name. Be creative, be original, be anything or anywhere you want—just don't let your pet be nameless.

How About . . .

Antarctica

Asia

Barcelona

Broadway

Brooklyn

Cairo

Fiji

Georgia

Kitty Hawk

Memphis

Paris

Tokyo

Locations and Places

Acapulco (Mexico)

Africa

Alamo (Texas)

Albany

Amazon (a river in South America)

America

Angola

Antarctica

Asia

Aspen (Colorado)

Austin (Texas)

Azores

Bahamas

Bali

Baltic

Bangkok (Thailand)

Bangladesh

Barbados

Barcelona

Bayou (a marshy creek)

Beijing (China)

Belgium

Belize

Bermuda

Bogota (Colombia)

Bombay

Boston

Brazil

Brazos (a river in Texas)

Broadway (the "Great White Way" in New York City)

Brooklyn (New York)

Burgundy (a region in France)

Burma

Butte (Montana)

Cairo (Eygpt)

Calgary (Canada)

Camelot (the legendary capital of Arthur's kingdom)

Cancun (Mexico)

Carmel (California)

Carolina

Cayman (Islands)

Chad

Chelsea (a district in London and in New York City)

Cheyenne (Wyoming)

Chile

China

Colorado (Rado)

Congo

Cozumel (Mexico)

D. C. (Washington, District of Columbia)

Dakota

Dallas (Texas)

Delaware (Dele)

Denmark

Denver

Dixie (a traditional name for the South)

Downtown

Egypt

El Dorado (the legendary City of Gold of the Spanish explorers)

Fargo (North Dakota)

Fiji

Florida

France

Freeway (a limited-access highway)

Fresno (California)

Gabon

Geneva

Georgia

Ghana

Granada

Greece

Guinea

Guyana

Hawaii

Hilton (a hotel chain)

Holland (The Netherlands)

Houston

Hyatt (a hotel chain)

India

Ixtapa (Mexico)

Jakarta

Jamaica

Jordan

Juneau (Alaska)

Junk Yard Cat

Junk Yard Dog

K. C. (Kansas City, Kansas and Missouri)

Katamandu (Nepal)

Kaunai

Kenya

Keys (a chain of islands off the southern tip of Florida)

Kitty Hawk

Klondike

Kong (Hong Kong)

L. A. (Los Angeles, California)

Locations and Places

Laos

Libya

Loch Ness (Scotland)

London

Madison

Madrid (Spain)

Mali

Malta

Manzanillo (Mexico)

Marriott (a hotel chain)

Maui

Mazatlan (Mexico)

Memphis (Tennessee)

Monaco

Montana

Morocco

Nassau

Nepal

Nevada

Nieman Marcus (an upscale department store)

Niger

Nile (a river in East Africa)

Oahu

Oman

Osaka

Oslo (Norway)

P. V. (Puerto Vallarta, Mexico)

Palau

Panama

Paris

Pecos (Texas)

Peking (China)

Persia

Peru

Phoenix (Arizona)

Pompeii

Rado (Colorado)

EUROPEAN VACATION . . .	
Amsterdam	London
Belgium	Madrid
Chelsea	Pompeii
Denmark	Rome
Geneva	Venice
Holland	Wales
Loch Ness	

Randolph

Reno

Reykjavik (Iceland)

Rio (Rio de Janeiro, Brazil)

Ritz (a luxury hotel)

Samoa

Sedona (a city in Arizona)

Seoul

Shade

Shiloh (the name for cities in Tennessee and Palestine)

Siam

Sidney (Australia)

Sierra

Spain

Sudan

Tahiti

Taipei

Taj Mahal (an Islamic monument built in India in the seventeenth century)

Tara (a village in Ireland)

Terlingua (a town in Texas)

Texas (Tex)

Tianjin

Tibet

Timbuktu (a city in Mali)

Togo (an African nation)

Tokyo

Tonga

Touraine (France)

Tripoli (Libya)

Troy (New York)

Tulsa

Turkey

Tuvalu

Uganda

Utah

Vegas (Las Vegas, Nevada)

Venice (Italy)

Virginia

Waco (Texas)

Wales

Yemen

Yukon

Yuma (Arizona)

Zaire

Zambia

"Fraidy"

13

Unusual Names and Nicknames

One of my clients once told me she had considered renaming her dog after she found herself standing in her front yard, at midnight, calling "Here, Woogie Woogie!"

But if you're not likely to be concerned with what other people think, feel free to get as outrageous as your imagination will allow.

How About . . .

BARKS A Lot

OH No

BAd DEbt

RiNKEY DiNK

CAPOOCHiNO

TWiNKlE TOES

JUStA CAt

Unusual Names and Nicknames

A. J.	Bark-ley	Billy Bob	Booker
AboGato	Bartender	Bingo	Boomer
Ace	Bartholo-mew	Binky	Boots
Al Fresco	Beau Beau	Blackjack	Bootsie
Al Poochino	Beaux	Blaze	Boozer
Alfie	Bebe	Bliss	Bowser
Alley Cat	Bee	Blitz	Boy
Allie	Belle	Blood	Boy Dog
Alpha	Beta	Blowout	Boz
Animal	Bif	Blue	Bozo
Apache	Big Boss	Bluegrass	Bravo
April	Big Boy	Bo	Briana
Arlee	Big Daddy	Bobbi	Bro
Aztec	Big Foot	Bobby	Bubah
B. B.	Big Guy	Bobo	Bubba
B. J.	Big John	Bomber	Bubbles
Babbs	Big Red	Boo	Buck
Baccarat	Big'un	BooBoo	Buckaroo
Backgammon	Bigbird	Boogie	Bucko
Ballerino	Bigun	Boogie Boy	Buckshot
Bandi	Bill Bailey	Booh	Bucky

Bud	Callie	Chancy	Chief
Buddy	Cally	Chap	Chilla
Buddyweiser	Candi	Chapin	Chimpy
Buffer	Cappy	Chappy	Chip
Buffin	Caprice	Chaps	Chris
Buffy	Captain Happy	Charlette	Chrisitiana
Bugsy	Card	Charley	Chrissy
Bullet	Career Girl	Charli	Christabel
Bun Bun	Cat #1	Charlie	Christmas
Buster	Cat #2	Charmin	Chu Chen
Buster Black	Cat Astrophe	Cheebe	Chu Chu
Butch	Cati	Cheers	Chuckles
Butterfingers	Catpuccino	Chelsea	Chula
Butthead	Catrinka	Chelsey	Chump
Button(s)	Catsanova	Chelsia	Chuska
Buzz	Catty Wompus	Chelsie	Cici
Ca Cee	Cee Gee	Cheri	Cinder
Cadi	Cha Cha	Cherokee	Cio Cio Sam
Cai	Chainsaw	Chew-chee	Cisco
Cali	Chamois	Chickie	Claus
Calley	Chance	Chicle	Clawdius

Unusual Names and Nicknames

Clazy	Cue Ball	Disco	Dweebe
Club	Cuki	Dobie	Dy
Co Co	D. C.	Dobie Won Kanobi	Elkie
Coco	D. D.		Esti
Coco Bear	D. J.	Doc	Eulika
Codie	Daffy	Donation	Ewoke
Cody	Dagney	Doo Dah	Exxene
Collie	Dahli	Doodle	Farkle
Comanche	Danny Boy	Doodles	Fella
Cooler	Dar	Doogie Bowser	Ferret Fawcett
Corker	Dawg	Doozie	Fifi
Corky	Dax	Dough Boy	Fila
Cotton	Daze	Doxy	Flakes
Cottontail	Dealer	Dude	Flaps
Cowboy	Deli	Dudette	Floorman
Crash	Destiny	Dudlee	Flower
Cribbage	Dexter	Duffie	Fluffer
Cricket	Diamond	Duffy	Fluffles
Critter	Dice	Dumpster	Flush
Crockett Cat	Digi (Digital)	Duster	Fragment
Crystal	Dingbat	Dusty	Fraidy
		Dutch	

Freebee	Grrrr	J. J.	Jukie
Friday	H. T.	Jackpot	Jumbo
Fusby	Hailey	Jammer	Just A Minute
G'Day	Half Pint	Jane Doe	Justa Cat
Ged	Hamlet	Jasmine	Justa Dog
Ghillie	Hawg	Jazz	Justice
Gi Gi	Hazard	Jenn-i-purr	Justin Time
Gig 'Em	Hef	Jetta	K. C.
Gin Rummy	Hekter	Jillsy	K. D.
Gink	Helen Dalmatian	Jimbo	K. J.
Girl	Hi Pockets	Jingles	Kadee
Girl Dog	Hissy Fit	Jinx	Kali
Gizmo	Hojo	Jip	Kally
Goober	Holly Hobbles	Jitter Bug	Kat
Goofie Bear	Hooter	Jive	Kater
Gorbe Chow	Howie	Jo Jo	Keba
Grammar	Iggy	Joe Cool	Keesha
Gringo	Ima Cat	Joker	Keeta
Grommet	Inca	Jossie	Kelli
Groove Dog	Itty Bitty	Jr.	Keno
Groovey	J. D.	Judi	Ker Plop

Unusual Names and Nicknames

Kevin Bacon

Key Key

Keys

Kiki

Kinki

Kit Kat

Kitsy

Kitt

Kittens

Kitter

Kitti

Kitty Boy

Kitty Carlyle

Kitty Q

Kitty Tom

Knuckles

Kobi

Kodak

Kokomo

Kringles

Kristil

Kuchen

Kwik

Kyrie

Lace

Lacey

Ladi

Lady Gal

Lady Lin

Lappy

Lawyer

Legacy

Lexie

Li'l Guy

Li'l Honeysuckle

Lia

Liberace

Little B

Little Bit

Little Girl

Little Kitty

Lobo

Lolo

Lotto

Lou Lou

Lutino

Mac Duff

Maci

Mackie

Maddie

MagnifiCat

Mail

Majic

Mama Trouble

Manager

Mao Tse Tongue

Mary Dog

Mate

Matey

Maudie

Maverick

Maxi

Mc Gruffen

Me Too

Meathead

Meetsie

Meow

Meow Say Tongue

Mercy

Merry Christmas

Mew

Mew Mew

Mia Ferret

Middie

Miffy

Milo

Mimi

Mimie

Minnesota Cats

Minni

Minnie

Minnie Paws

Miss Behavin'

Miss Chevious

Miss Demeanor	Mopsy	Mutzie	Paw Pet
Miss Fortune	Mortikie	Navajo	Payout
Miss Kitty	Morty	New Kitty	Peace
Miss Take	Moss	Nic Nac	Pebbles
Miss Tickle	Mouse Tse Tung	Nicky	Pee Dee
Missy	Mr. Cuddles	Niki	Pennie
Misty	Mr. Kitty	Nikke	Penny
Mitch	Mr. Stubbs	No White	Peppy
Mitzi	Mr. T	Nooner	Perky
Mitzie	Mrs. T	Odd Ball	Petunia
Mitzu	Ms. Muffet	Okie	Phideaux
Mixture	Mudd	Ombre	PiCatSo
Mo	Muff	Owlpuccino	Pilot
Mo Jo	Muffer	P. B.	Pinky
Moe	Muffett	P. C.	Pitney
Moffie	Muffie	P. C. Jr.	Player
Mofford	Muffy	P. J.	Podnah
Molley	Muggs	Pandy	Pojoo
Moma	Mugsie	Papito	Poker
Momma Dog (Cat)	Mugsly	Papoose	Polecat
Moo Moo	Munchkin	Paraphernalia (Pari)	Poli

Unusual Names and Nicknames

Polson	Prof	Puss	Ringo
Ponch	Pucci	Puss Cat	Rip
Poo Bee Bear	Pudder	Putty Tat	Rip Van Beagle
Pooch	Puddy Willow	R. B.	Rock
Poochie	Puffy	Rags	Rockey
Poochkie	Pugsly	Rainbow	Rock-ola
Pooh	Punkie	Ralfy	Rodeo
Pooh Bear	Punky	Rascal	Rolf
Pooky	Pup	Rasta	Rollie
Pooper	Pupdog	Rat	Romer
Poops	Pupper	Ratcat	Roo
Pooter	Puppy	Ratus	Rootin' Tootin
Poppy	Pups	Raven	Rosco
Potsi	Pupster	Razz	Roscoe
Pozzo	Pupus	Razzy	Rose
Primadonna	Purr	Recount	Rosebud
Princess Daisy	Purr Son	Red Neck	Rosie
Princess Josette	Purrbert	Reel	Roxie
Princess Tiffany	Purrsilla	Reggie	Roxy
Priss	Purrsnickitty	Remington	Rug Rat
Prissy	Purse	Ricki	Ruffles

S. L. O'Pokey

Saddle

Saige

Sailor

Saint Bernie Nard

Samba (o)

Sami

Sarg

Sashi

Sassy

Sassy San

Saturday

Saucer

Sawdust

Scamp

Scat Cat

Schwatz

Scottie

Scrabble

Sebo

Seminole

Serendipity

Sergeant Pepper

Shadie

Shady

Shammy

Sheba

Sheeba

Shimmy

Shinola

Shoebutton

Shooter

Shorty Bob

Shotie

Shotz

Shu Shu

Shy Ann

Si

Siah

Silver Bell

Sioux

Sir Chadwick

Sir Woody

Sissie

Sissy

Sister

Skeeter

Skinner

Skipper

Skippy

Skitter

Skitty

Skunky

Skwiggles

Skye

Slick

Slot

Slugger

Smitty

Snapper de Aire

Snert

Snoobie

Snooker

Snooky

Snoops

Snow Bear

Snowball

Snubbs

Snuff

Sonny

Soo

Soo Shi

Sooka

Sophistocat

SoSueMe

Spade

Sparky

Special

Speckles

Speed Bump

Spike

Spiker

Spikey

Spin

Unusual Names and Nicknames

Spirit	Star	Stud	Tango
Splash	Stardust	Stymie	Tashi
Split	Starr	Sudi	Tasi
Spooner	Stash	Su-Lin	Taski
Sport	Static	Sue E.	Tatters
Sporty	Sterling	Suki	Tattoo
Spring	Stickers	Sundance	Tawnya
Sprinkle	Stimey	Sunday	Taz
Spunky	Stinker	Sunnie	Ted E. Bear
Squeaker	Stoney	Sunny	Tennie
Squeakers	Stormy	Sunny Cat	Tex
Squealer	Striker	Sunspot	Thomas Our Cat
Squish	Strubie	Supplies	Thunder
		Suzie Queen	Tic Tac
		T. C.	Tick Tock
		T. J.	Ticker
		Taboo	Tidbit
		Taffi	Tiffy
		TAG Heuer	Tikki
		Tai	Tiko
		Tally	Timex

"Splash"

Tinker	Tracer	Wagley	Wild Thing
Tippy	Trapper	Wakedy Yak	Wildfire
Tipster	Trendsetter	Wallin' Jennings	Willow
Tipsy	Trifecta	Waterford	Wimpy
Tobe	Trixie	Way Out Willie	Winkie
Tobi	Trooper	Weebles	Winner
Tobia	Trouffels	Wetta	Wisky Blue
Toddy	Trucker	Whacker	Wizard
Tomahawk	Tuffy	Whampuss	Woodsie
Tom Dooley	Turbo	Whiplash	Woogy
Toodles	Turkey	Whisper	Woopsie
Toot	Tusche	Whiz Bang	Wova
Toot Toot	Twerp	Whiz O	Wrecks
Tootie	Twinkle Toes	Why Not	YoYo
Tootsie	Twit	Wicked Wizard	Zac
Topper	Tynee	Wicket	Zee
Torti	Uga	Wifferdill	Zero
Tortilla	Velcro	Wild Child	Zip

14

Cartoon Characters

Your pet may be the perfect Daffy Duck or Road Runner—guaranteed to always make you laugh. But plan ahead! When he or she is testing your patience, a stern "Jughead, I told you to behave" may change your stern countenance into a smiling face.

How About . . .

Angelica Pickles

Donald Duck

Ash

Heifer

Bugs Bunny

Cartoon Characters

ORIGINAL LOONEY TUNES

Bugs Bunny
Mischievous bunny.

Daffy Duck
Sometimes-enemy of Bugs Bunny.

Elmer Fudd
A hunter in *Looney Tunes* who is always trying to catch Bugs Bunny.

Pepe Le Pew
A skunk character in *Looney Tunes*.

Porky Pig
A character in *Looney Tunes*.

Road Runner
A character in *Looney Tunes* who constantly evades Wile E. Coyote.

Sylvester the Cat
A black-and-white cat who has appeared often with Tweety Pie, the canary, in many Warner Brothers' animated cartoons.

Tasmanian Devil
A crazed character in the original *Looney Tunes*.

Wile E. Coyote
Coyote who hunts the Road Runner, but can never quite catch him.

THE FLINSTONES

Bam Bam
Fred and Betty's son.

Barney Rubble
Best friend and neighbor of Fred.

Betty Rubble
Barney's wife.

Fred Flinstone
Main character and husband of Wilma.

Pebbles
Fred and Wilma's daughter.

Wilma Flinstone
Fred's wife.

NICKELODEON CLASSICS

Angelica Pickles
Main antagonist and older cousin of Tommy Pickles in *Rugrats*.

Chucky Finster
Main character's best friend and scaredy cat in *Rugrats*.

Doug
Title character.

Heifer

A cow raised by wolves in *Rocko's Modern Life*.

Ickus

Character in *Real Monsters*.

Krumb

Character in *Real Monsters*.

Lil

Phil's twin in *Rugrats*.

Oblina

One of the three main monsters in *Real Monsters*.

Patrick Star

SpongeBob's starfish pal.

Phil

Lil's twin in *Rugrats*.

Philbert

A turtle in *Rocko's Modern Life*.

Porkchop

Faithful dog in the series *Doug*.

Rocko

An Australian wallaby and title character in *Rocko's Modern Life*.

Skeeter

Doug's best friend in the cartoon series.

SpongeBob SquarePants

A pants-wearing sponge who is the title character of the animated series.

Squidward Tentacles

An unfriendly neighborhood squid on *SpongeBob SquarePants*.

Tommy Pickles

Leader of the group of babies in *Rugrats*.

MORE CARTOON CHARACTERS

Al Capp

Cartoonist; creator of "Li'l Abner."

Albert

A main character in "Pogo." Also the name of the title character in the T.V. series *Fat Albert*.

Alley Oop

Title character.

Alvin

A character in *The Chipmunks*.

Andy Capp

Title character.

Animal Crackers

Title character.

Annie (Little Orphan)

Title character.

Cartoon Characters

Archie
Title character.

Ash
Main character in the popular cartoon *Pokemon*.

B. C.
Title character.

Barney Google
Title character.

Bart Simpson
Character in *The Simpsons*.

Batman
Title character.

Beetle Bailey
Title character.

Beauregard Bugleboy
A character in "POGO."

Beavis
Title character in *Beavis and Butthead*.

Bender
Animated robot on the television series *Futurama*.

Betty Boop
Title character.

Blondie
Title character.

Blossom
Leader of *The Powerpuff Girls*, an animated series.

Bluto
Character in *Popeye*.

Bobby Hill
Peggy and Hank's son on *King of the Hill*.

Bonzo
Title character.

Boris
Character in *Rocky and Bullwinkle*.

Brainey
A character in *The Smurfs*.

Brutus
A villain in *Popeye*.

Bubbles
One of *The Powerpuff Girls*.

Bullwinkle Moose
Title character in *Rocky and Bullwinkle*.

Bumstead
DAGWOOD and BLONDIE'S family name.

Buster Brown
Title character.

Buttercup
Another of *The Powerpuff Girls*.

Butthead
Title character in *Beavis and Butthead*.

Buzz Sawyer
Title character.

Calvin
Title character in "Calvin and Hobbes."

Cap Stubbs
Title character.

Captain Marvel
Title character.

Casper
Title character: *Casper the Friendly Ghost*.

Cathy
Title character.

Charlie Brown
Co-star of comic strip and television series *Peanuts*.

Chef (McElroy)
The school chef voiced by Isaac Hayes on *South Park*.

Chip
Title character in *Chip and Dale*.

Chipmunk(s)
Title character(s).

Dagwood
BLONDIE'S husband.

Daisy
DONALD DUCK'S girlfriend.

Daisy Mae
LI'L ABNER'S girlfriend.

CHILDHOOD HEROES . . .	
Blossom	**Garfield**
Bullwinkle	**Gumby**
Buttercup	**Huckleberry Hound**
Captain Marvel	**Mighty Mouse**
Charlie Brown	**Rocky**
Dennis the Menace	**Scooby Doo**
Donald Duck	**Winnie-the-Pooh**
Dora	**Woodstock**

Cartoon Characters

Dale
Title character in *Chip and Dale*.

Dennis the Menace
Title character.

Deputy Dawg
Title character.

Dewey
Character in "Donald Duck."

Dick Tracy
Title character.

Diego
Character in the animated TV series *Dora the Explorer*.

Dilbert
Title character.

Dinny
ALLEY OOP'S pet dinosaur.

Dipsy
A character in the TV comic series *Teletubbies*.

Donald Duck
Title character; also MICKEY MOUSE'S friend.

Doonesbury
Title of strip.

Dora
The title character in the animated TV series *Dora the Explorer*.

Droopy
Title character.

Elwood
Title character.

Farley
Dog in the comic strip "For Better or Worse."

Fearless Fosdick
Character in "Li'l Abner."

Felix the Cat
Title character.

Flash Gordon
Title character.

Fred Basset
Title character.

Fritz
A character in "The Katzenjammer Kids."

Fritz the Cat
Title character.

Garfield
Title character.

Gertie

Title character in "Gertie, the Trained Dinosaur."

Goofy

A character in "Mickey Mouse."

Gordo

Title character.

Grammy

Title character.

Gumby

Title character in *Gumby and Pokey*.

Gummi Bear

Title character.

Hagar the Horrible

Title character.

Hank Hill

Texan father voiced by Mike Judge on *King of the Hill*.

Hans

A character in "The Katzenjammer Kids."

Happy Hooligan

Title character.

Hazel

Title character.

Heathcliff

Title character.

Heckle and Jeckle

Title characters.

Henry

Title character.

Hi

Title character of "Hi and Lois."

Hobbes

Title character in "Calvin and Hobbes."

Homer Simpson

Character in *The Simpsons*.

Huckleberry Hound

The hero of the first all-animated television series, *Huckleberry Hound*, created by Hanna-Barbera Productions in 1958.

Huey

Character in "Donald Duck."

Ignatz Mouse

Title character.

Jeff

Title character in "Mutt and Jeff."

Jerry

Title character in *Tom and Jerry*.

Cartoon Characters

Jiggs

A character in the cartoon strip "Bringing Up Father."

Joe Cool

SNOOPY's alter ego in *Peanuts*.

Joe Palooka

Title character.

Jughead

A character in "Archie."

Jungle Jim

Title character.

Katzenjammer Kids

Title character(s).

Kenny McCormick

The small boy who dies at the end of every episode of *South Park*.

Krazy Kat

Title character.

Laa-Laa

A character in the TV comic series *Teletubbies*.

Li'l Abner

Title character.

Linus

A character in the comic strip and television series *Peanuts*.

Lisa Simpson

Character in *The Simpsons*.

Little Lulu

Title character.

Lois

Title character in "Hi and Lois."

Louie

Character in "Donald Duck."

Luann

Title character.

Lucy

A character in *Peanuts*.

CARTOON CHARACTERS FOR BIG KIDS . . .

Bart Simpson	Kenny McCormick
Beavis	Lisa Simpson
Butthead	Marge Simpson
Chef	Peter Griffin
Hank Hill	Smithers
Homer Simpson	Stewie

Margaret
A character in "Dennis the Menace."

Marge Simpson
Character in *The Simpsons*.

Marmaduke
Title character.

Mickey Mouse
Title character.

Mighty Mouse
Title character.

Minnie Mouse
MICKEY MOUSE'S girlfriend.

Mojo Jojo
The archenemy of *The Powerpuff Girls*.

Moon Mullins
Title character.

Mr. Boffo
Title character.

Mr. Magoo
Title character.

Muddy the Mudskipper
Character in *Ren and Stimpy*.

Mutt
Title character in "Mutt and Jeff."

Nancy
Title character.

Napoleon
Title character.

Natasha
Character in *Rocky and Bullwinkle*.

Nermal
Cat in "Garfield" comics.

Nervy Nat
Title character.

Noo-Noo
A character in the TV comic series *Teletubbies*.

Nudnik
Title character.

Odie
GARFIELD'S canine friend.

Offisa Bull Pupp
A character in *Krazy Kat*.

Okefenokee
The setting (a swamp) in the series "Pogo."

Olive Oil
POPEYE'S girlfriend.

Cartoon Characters

Opus
The penguin in the comic strip series "Bloom County."

Pasquale
Baby boy in the comic strip "Rose is Rose."

Peanuts
Title of comic strip and television series.

Peggy Hill
Texan mother on *King of the Hill*.

Pepe Le Pu
Title character.

Peppermint Patty
A character in the comic strip and television series *Peanuts*.

Peter Griffin
Father and one of the main characters in *Family Guy*.

Petunia Pig
A character in "Porky Pig."

Phineas T. Bridgeport
A character in "Pogo."

Pig-Pen
A character in the comic strip and television series *Peanuts*.

Pikachu
Pokemon and Ash's companion in the series *Pokemon*.

Pink Panther
Title character.

Pluto
MICKEY MOUSE'S dog.

Po
A character in the TV comic series *Teletubbies*.

Pogo
Title character.

Pokey
Title character in *Gumby and Pokey*.

Popeye
Title character.

Porky Pig
Title character.

Prince Valiant
Title character.

Professor Utonium
Creator/father figure to *The Powerpuff Girls*.

Quincy
The iguana in the comic strip "Fox Trot."

Ready
Title character in "Ruff and Ready."

Ren
The skinny chihuahua on *Ren and Stimpy*.

Rocky (the Flying Squirrel)
Title character in *Rocky and Bullwinkle*.

Rose
Title character in "Rose is Rose."

Ruff
(1) A character in "Dennis the Menace"; (2) title character in "Ruff and Ready."

Sally
A character in the comic strip and television series *Peanuts*.

Schroeder
A character in the comic strip and television series *Peanuts*.

Scooby Doo
Title character.

Simon
Title character, *The Chipmunks*.

Simple J. Malarkey
A character in "Pogo."

Sluggo
(1) Sarge's dog in the comic strip "Beetle Bailey." (2) NANCY'S friend in "Nancy."

Smithers
Character in *The Simpsons*.

Smurf
Title character.

Smurfette
A character in *The Smurfs*.

Snoopy
Title character in the comic strip and television series *Peanuts*.

Cartoon Characters

Snuffy Smith
Title character.

Solomon
Title character.

Space Ghost
Title character.

Speedy Gonzales
Title character.

Spike
A character in *Tom and Jerry*; a character in *Rugrats*.

Steve Canyon
Title character.

Stewie
The conniving and British baby in *Family Guy*.

Stimpy
The cat voiced by Billy West in *Ren and Stimpy*.

Stinky
Character in *Doug*.

Sweet Pea
Character in "Popeye."

Sylvester
Title character.

Sylvia
Title character.

Tarzan
Title character.

Tinky Winky
A character in the TV comic series *Teletubbies*.

Tintin
Title character.

Tippie
Title character in a comic strip no longer in print.

Tom
Title character in *Tom and Jerry*.

Trudy
Title character.

Tweetie Pie
A character in the comic strip and animated cartoon *Sylvester the Cat*.

Veronica
A character in "Archie."

Wiley Catt
A character in "Pogo."

Wimpie

A character in the comic strip and animated cartoon *Popeye*.

Winnie-the-Pooh

Title character.

Wizard of Id

Title character.

Woodstock

A character in the comic strip and television series *Peanuts*.

Woody the Woodpecker

Title character.

Yogi (Bear)

The hero of the animated television cartoon *Yogi Bear*, who lives in Jellystone National Park.

Zero

A character in "Beetle Bailey."

Ziggy

Title character.

"Peter, Paul, & Mary"

15

Entertainers/Musicians/ Pop Culture

A singer or entertainer may become your new pet's name. Use this short chapter to give you some ideas; there are only a few names suggested to get you started on your own list.

How About . . .

Barbra Streisand

Beyoncé

Bob Dylan

Carrie Underwood

David Letterman

Frank Sinatra

Miley Cyrus

Rihanna

Ryan Seacrest

Taylor Swift

Entertainers/Musicians/Pop Culture

ENTERTAINERS—PAST AND PRESENT

Adam Sandler

Alan Jackson

Barbara Mandrell

Barbra Streisand

B. B. King

Beatle(s)

Bee Gee(s)

Bette Midler

Beyoncé

Bill Cosby

Bill Murray

Billy Joel

Billy Ray Cyrus

Bing Crosby

Black Eyed Peas

Blood, Sweat and Tears

Bob Dylan

Bobbie Gentry

Bobby Goldsboro

Bob Hope

Bon Jovi

Bonnie Raitt

Brad Paisley

Brenda Lee

Bruce Springsteen

Buck Owens

Buddy Hackett

Buddy Holly

Carole King

Carrie Underwood

Charlie Daniels

Charlie Pride

Charlie Rich

Cher

Chet Atkins

Chris Brown

Chris Isaak

Chubby Checker

Chuck Berry

Clint Black

POP ICONS . . .

Beatles	Lady Gaga
Beyonce	Madonna
Britney Spears	Michael Jackson
Cher	Miley Cyrus
Hannah Montana	Rihanna
Jay-Z	Taylor Swift
Justin Timberlake	

Conan O'Brien	Eric Clapton	Hank Williams
Conway Twitty	Ernest Tubb	Hannah Montana
Crystal Gayle	Fleetwood Mac	Harpo Marx
Dale Evans	Floyd (Pink Floyd)	Harry Chapin
Dan Aykroyd	Floyd Cramer	Ingrid Michaelson
Dane Cook	Frank Sinatra	Jack Benny
David Copperfield	Frankie Avalon	James Taylor
David Bowie	Fred Astaire	Jay Leno
David Letterman	Gallagher	Jay-Z
Dean Martin	Garth Brooks	Jerry Lewis
Diana Ross	Gene Autry	Jerry Lee Lewis
Dolly Parton	Gene Kelly	Jerry Seinfeld
Dottie West	George Burns	Jimmy Buffett
Drake	George Carlin	Joan Baez
Dusty Springfield	George Harrison	Joan Rivers
Dwight Yoakam	George Strait	Jimmy Dean
Eagle(s)	Gilda Radner	John Denver
Eddie Murphy	Glen Campbell	Johnny Cash
Elton John	Gracie Allen	Judy Collins
Elvis Presley	Groucho Marx	Judy Garland
Emmylou Harris	Hank Snow	Julio Iglesias

June Carter	Madonna	Patty Loveless
Kanye West	Marie Osmond	Paul Anka
Katy Perry	Marshal Mathers	Paul Simon
Keith Urban	Martha McBride	Paul McCartney
Kelly Clarkson	Marty Robbins	Pavarotti
Kenny Chesney	Mel Tillis	Peter, Paul & Mary
Kenny Rogers	Merle Haggard	Phil Collins
Kris Kristofferson	Merle Travis	Randy Travis
Lady Gaga	Michael Bolton	Ray Charles
Lawrence Welk	Michael Jackson	Ray Price
Lee Greenwood	Mick Jagger	Ray Stevens
Lily Tomlin	Miley Cyrus	Reba McEntire
Linda Ronstadt	Milton Berle	Red Buttons
Liberace	Naomi Judd	Red Skelton
Lionel Richie	Natalie Cole	Regina Spector
Liza Minnelli	Nat "King" Cole	Ricky Van Shelton
Loretta Lynn	Neil Sedaka	Rihanna
Louis Armstrong	Olivia Newton-John	Ringo Starr
Lyle Lovett	Otis Redding	Rod Stewart
Lynn Anderson	Paramore	Robert Earl Keen
Mac Davis	Patsy Cline	Ronnie Milsap

Roseanne Cash

Roy Acuff

Roy Clark

Roy Orbison

Roy Rogers

Ryan Seacrest

Sam Cooke

Sammy Davis Jr.

Selena

Simon Cowell

Sonny Bono

Steely Dan

Stevie Ray Vaughn

Stevie Wonder

Tanya Tucker

Taylor Swift

Tennessee Ernie Ford

Tex Ritter

Tim McGraw

Tina Fey

Tina Turner

Tom T. Hall

Tony Bennett

Travis Tritt

Trisha Yearwood

U2

Van Halen

Vince Gill

Waylon Jennings

Wayne Newton

Whitney Houston

Wilco

Wil.i.am

Willie Nelson

Wynonna Judd

"Taylor Swift"

COMPOSERS

Andrew Lloyd Webber
British composer (b. 1948).

Bach
German composer (1685–1750).

Beethoven
German composer (1770–1827).

Cole Porter
American composer (1893–1964).

George Gershwin
American composer (1898–1937).

Irving Berlin
American composer (1888–1989).

Mozart
Austrian composer (1756–1791).

Noel Coward
British composer (1899–1973).

FUNNY PEOPLE . . .	
Adam Sandler	David Letterman
Bette Midler	George Carlin
Bill Murray	Jay Leno
Conan O'Brien	Jerry Seinfeld
Dane Cook	Roseanne

"Beethoven"

"Derek Jeter"

16

Sports

Throughout the past century, sports has played a big part in our lives. Whether you are an avid sports buff or a part-time fan keeping up with your favorite team, consider some of these entries in your selection of your pet's name.

How About . . .

A Rod

Derek Jeter

Eli Manning

Kevin Garnett

Kobe Bryant

Michael Jordan

Serena Williams

Shaquille O'Neal

Steve Nash

Tiger Woods

Venus Williams

BASEBALL STARS AND TERMS

A Rod (Alex Rodriguez)

All-star third baseman for the New York Yankees. Considered one of the best players of all time.

Al Worthington

A pitcher for the Giants in the 50s and the Twins and the White Sox in the 60s.

Andruw Jones

Gold glove centerfielder, played for the Atlanta Braves, Los Angeles Dodgers, and Texas Rangers.

Aramis Ramirez

Third baseman for the Pittsburgh Pirates and Chicago Cubs.

Babe Ruth

One of the most famous all-time athletes, Ruth hit sixty home runs in 1927 while playing for the New York Yankees.

Balk

An incomplete or misleading motion.

Barry Bonds

Single season home run record holder. Winner of the Hank Aaron Award in 2001, 2002, and 2004.

Batter

The player attempting to hit the ball.

Boog Powell

Outfielder for the Baltimore Orioles in the 60s and 70s; best known for his appearance on Miller Lite beer commercials.

Cal Ripken

On September 6, 1995, broke Lou Gehrig's record of 2,130 for most consecutive games played.

Carlos Delgado

Power-hitting first baseman, played for the Toronto Blue Jays, Florida Marlins, and New York Mets.

Casey Stengel

Former manager of the New York Yankees; led his team to ten American League pennant titles from 1949 to 1980.

Catcher

The player who receives the pitches from the pitcher.

David Ortiz

Slugging first baseman, played for the Minnesota Twins and Boston Red Sox.

Derek Jeter

All-star long-time New York Yankee shortstop.

Dizzy Dean
Winner of National League's Most Valuable Player Award, 1934.

Ernie Banks
Hit 512 National League home runs.

Fastball
A PITCH thrown at a high rate of speed.

Fly Ball
A pitch that is hit high into the air.

Grounder
A ball hit on the ground by the BATTER.

Hank Aaron
Hall of Famer and holder of the following records: Home runs (1st), Runs scored (2nd), and Hits (3rd). In 1999 major league baseball instituted the Hank Aaron Award for the best hitters of the National and American Leagues.

Hit-and-Run
A play in which the runner progresses to the next base simultaneously with the BATTER hitting the PITCH.

Home Run
A play in which the ball hit by the BATTER allows him to proceed around all three bases safely to home plate.

Homer
See HOME RUN.

Joe DiMaggio
Former New York Yankees outfielder; hit safely in 56 consecutive baseball games.

Johnny Bench
Former catcher for the Cincinnati Reds; MVP twice.

Kevin Youkilis
Gold-glove winning first baseman for the Boston Red Sox.

Knuckleball
A pitch thrown by gripping the ball with the knuckles of two or three fingers.

Lou Gehrig
Hall of Famer; active from 1923 to 1939; one of the all-time greats.

Manny Ramirez
All-star power hitter, played for the Cleveland Indians, Boston Red Sox, and Los Angeles Dodgers.

Mark McGwire
Broke record for most home runs in a season—162 game season: 70 home runs while playing with the St. Louis Cardinals, NL, 1998, and again in 1999 when he hit 65 home runs.

Maury Wills

Los Angeles Dodgers' shortstop who set a record in 1962 by stealing 104 bases.

Mickey Mantle

New York Yankees outfielder who led the American League in home runs four seasons. During his career with the Yankees from 1952 to 1968, his team won eleven pennants and seven World Championships.

Nolan Ryan

Record holder for most number of lifetime strikeouts by a pitcher (broke 5,000 mark in 1989).

Pete Rose

Leader in total number of lifetime hits (4,256); played mostly with the Cincinnati Reds; suspended in 1989 for betting on baseball.

Pitch

The term used for the ball when it is thrown by the PITCHER to the BATTER.

Pitcher

One who throws the ball to the batter.

Pitchout

A PITCH deliberately thrown high and outside making it easy for the CATCHER to retrieve.

Prince Fielder

Power-hitting first baseman for the Milwaukee Brewers.

Reggie Jackson

American League home run champion 1973, 1975, and 1980.

Roger Maris

Former New York Yankees player; hit 61 home runs in 1961.

Runner

In baseball, the player who attempts to round the bases; also a person who jogs or runs.

Sacrifice

A play in which the BATTER is out but a RUNNER advances to another base.

Sammy Sosa

Hit 50 home runs in a season—162 game season Chicago, NL, 2000, one of the first winners of the Hank Aaron Award 1999.

Sandy Koufax

Los Angeles Dodgers pitcher who won the Cy Young Award in 1963, 1965, and 1966.

Shortstop

The position between second and third base.

Sparky Anderson

Manager of the Cincinnati Reds until 1979 at which time he became manager of the Detroit Tigers.

Stan Musial

Player for the St. Louis Cardinals in the 50s and 60s; a Hall of Famer, Musial held National League records for having played more games (3,026) than any other National Leaguer; he also held league records for most runs batted in, most at bats, most runs scored, and most base hits.

Strike

A PITCH that the BATTER misses.

Ted Williams

Hall of Famer; six time American League batting champion from 1939 to 1960.

Todd Helton

All-star slugging first baseman for the Colorado Rockies.

Ty Cobb

A Detroit Tigers' player in the early 1900s who had a lifetime batting average of .367 and 4,191 base hits. He was the first member of the National Baseball Hall of Fame.

Whitey Ford

New York Yankees pitcher in the 50s and 60s; holder of the following lifetime World Series records: most victories (pitcher), most innings pitched, most consecutive scoreless innings, and most strikeouts by pitcher.

Willie Mays

San Francisco Giants and New York Mets outfielder who had a career batting average of .302. His lifetime total of 660 homers was topped only by BABE RUTH and HANK AARON; Hall of Famer.

Yogi Berra

Hall of Famer; active 1946 to 1965. Holder of record number of hits (71) in World Series (lifetime).

BASKETBALL STARS AND TERMS

Allen Iverson

NBA MVP, played for the Philadelphia 76ers, Denver Nuggets, and Detroit Pistons.

Bob Cousy

A Boston Celtics standout, Cousy scored fifty points in a 1953 playoff game—a record at the time.

Charles Barkley
NBA MVP, played for the Phoenix Suns.

David Robinson
NBA Rookie of the Year in 1989–1990; 1991 rebound leader; NBA MVP in 1995, played for the San Antonio Spurs.

Dirk Nowitzki
NBA MVP, played for the Dallas Mavericks.

Dribble
Bouncing the ball on the floor.

Ervin Johnson
NBA MVP for 1990, played for the Los Angeles Lakers.

Hakeem Olajuwon
Played for the Houston Rockets, NBA MVP.

Hoop
The goal.

Julius Erving
Third lifetime NBA leading scorer (30,026 points through 1988 season).

Jump Shot
A play in which the ball is propelled toward the GOAL while the player is airborne.

Kareem Abdul-Jabbar
Lew Alcindor; Individual NBA scoring champion 1960 to 1972; Milwaukee Bucks.

Karl Malone
Utah NBA MVP for 1997 (Utah Jazz).

Kevin Garnett
NBA MVP 2003–04.

Kobe Bryant
NBA MVP 2007–08.

Larry Bird
High-scoring forward of the Boston Celtics; winner of the NBA Most Valuable Player Award, 1984.

Layup
A shot made by playing the ball off the backboard from close to the basket, usually after driving in.

Magic Johnson
Winner of the NBA Most Valuable Player Award, 1987; member of the Los Angeles Lakers.

Michael Jordan
NBA individual scoring champion 1986 to 1988 and NBA MVP in 1991, 1992, 1996, and 1998 (Chicago Bulls).

Moses Malone

NBA leader in free throws.

Pistol Pete Maravich

Holder of two college top single-game scoring records: 1969 (66 points); 1970 (69 points); also leading individual NBA scorer in 1976 to 1977 (2,273 points).

Rebound

The act of retrieving and recovering the ball after a missed shot.

Red Auerbach

Former coach of the Boston Celtics.

Shaquille O'Neal

Orlando Magic star who was the 1995 scoring leader and NBA MVP in 2000 with the Los Angeles Lakers.

Sky Hook

A hook shot that attains more than usual height.

Slam Dunk

The maneuver in which a player forces the ball into the net from above the rim.

Steve Nash

NBA MVP 2004–2005, 2005–2006.

Swish

A shot that passes through the rim without touching it.

"Slam Dunk"

Tim Duncan

NBA Rookie of the Year 1997–1998 and MVP for 2001–2002, 2002–2003 (San Antonio Spurs).

Wilt Chamberlain

Star of the Philadelphia Warriors and the Los Angeles Lakers, scoring a record 100 points in one game. He averaged 50.4 points per game during the 1961–1962 season.

FOOTBALL STARS AND TERMS

Andre Ware
1989 winner of the Heisman Trophy.

Archie Griffin
1974 and 1975 winner of the Heisman Trophy (Ohio State University).

Barry Sanders
1988 winner of the Heisman Trophy (Oklahoma State University).

MVPs . . .	
Alan Iverson	John Elway
Brett Hull	Kevin Garnett,
Charles Barkley	Kobe Bryant
Chris Pronger	Peyton Manning
David Robinson	Ray Lewis
Deion Branch	Santonio Holmes
Eli Manning	Shaquille O'Neal
Emmitt Smith	Steve Nash
Ervin Johnson	Tom Brady
Joe Montana	

Bart Starr
Hall of Famer; active 1965 to 1973; associated mainly with the Green Bay Packers.

Bear Bryant
Coach at Texas A&M University in the 50s and at the University of Alabama in the 60s, 70s, and 80s.

Billy Sims
1978 winner of the Heisman Trophy.

Bobby Mitchell
First black player to be a member of the Washington Redskins; he was later elected to the Hall of Fame.

Carson Palmer
Winner of the 2002 Heisman Trophy (USC).

Center
In football, the player who hands the ball to the QUARTERBACK.

Charles White
1979 winner of the Heisman Trophy (USC).

Charles Woodson
Winner of the 1997 Heisman Trophy (Michigan).

Charley Taylor
A receiver for the Washington Redskins who caught a record 649 passes from 1964 to 1977.

Charlie Ward
1993 winner of the Heisman Trophy (Florida State University).

Chris Weinke
Winner of the 2000 Heisman Trophy (Florida State).

Dan Marino
American Hall of Fame player; one of the most prolific quarterbacks in league history, holding or having held almost every major NFL passing record.

Danny Wuerffel
Winner of the 1996 Heisman Trophy (Florida).

Deion Branch
MVP of the 2004 Super Bowl.

Desmond Howard
1991 winner of the Heisman Trophy (Michigan); NFL Super Bowl MVP in 1996.

Dexter Jackson
MVP of the 2002 Super Bowl.

Dick Butkus
Hall of Famer; active 1965 to 1973; associated mainly with Chicago Bears.

Doug Flutie
1984 Heisman Trophy winner (Boston College).

Earl Campbell
1977 Heisman Trophy winner (University of Texas).

Eddie George
1995 winner of the Heisman Trophy (Ohio State).

Eli Manning
MVP of the 2007 Super Bowl.

Emmitt Smith
All-time NFL rushing leader and NFL Super Bowl MVP in 1993.

Eric Crouch
Winner of the 2001 Heisman Trophy (Nebraska).

Extra Point
Scoring a point after a TOUCHDOWN.

Fullback
A player in the BACKFIELD.

Fumble

The act of an offensive ball carrier dropping the ball.

George Rogers

1980 winner of the Heisman Trophy (South Carolina).

Gino Torretta

1992 winner of the Heisman Trophy (Miami).

Halfback

A player in the BACKFIELD.

Hand-off

One offensive player giving the ball to another offensive player.

Herschel Walker

1982 Heisman Trophy winner (University of Georgia).

Hines Ward

MVP of the 2005 Super Bowl.

Interception

A play in which a defensive player catches a pass in the air.

Jason White

Winner of the 2003 Heisman Trophy (Oklahoma).

Jerry Rice

NFL Super Bowl MVP in 1988.

Jim Brown

Professional football Hall of Famer; Cleveland Browns, 1957 to 1965.

Joe Montana

Three-time MVP of Super Bowl Championship teams.

Joe Namath

The New York Jets quarterback and Hall of Famer (1985); led his team to a 16–7 victory over the Baltimore Colts in the 1969 Super Bowl.

John Elway

NFL Super Bowl MVP in 1998.

Kickoff

Putting the ball into play by kicking it to the opposing team from a stationary position on the ground.

Kurt Warner

NFL Super Bowl MVP in 1999.

Larry Brown

NFL Super Bowl MVP in 1996.

Marcus Allen

1981 winner of the Heisman Trophy (USC).

Mark Rypien
NFL Super Bowl MVP in 1992.

Matt Leinart
Winner of the 2004 Heisman Trophy
(USC).

Mike Ditka
Coach of the 1985 Super Bowl Champion
Chicago Bears.

Mike Rozier
1983 winner of the Heisman Trophy
(Nebraska).

Ottis Anderson
NFL Super Bowl MVP in 1990.

Peyton Manning
MVP of the 2005 Super Bowl.

Punt
A kick in which the ball is kicked when
dropped from the hands before it touches
the ground.

Quarterback
The player who receives the ball from the
CENTER, calls the signals, and directs the
offensive plays of the team.

Rashaan Salaam
1994 winner of the Heisman Trophy
(Colorado).

Ray Lewis
NFL Super Bowl MVP in 2000.

Recovery
The act of regaining possession of the ball
after a fumble.

Red Grange
Illinois University player in the 1920s; he
was known as "The Galloping Ghost."

Reggie Bush
Winner of the 2005 Heisman Trophy
(USC).

Ricky Williams
Winner of the 1998 Heisman Trophy
(Texas).

Ron Dayne
Winner of the 1999 Heisman Trophy
(Wisconsin).

Safety
The grounding of the ball by the offensive
team behind its own goal line; a defensive
player farthest from the line of SCRIMMAGE.

Sam Bradford
Winner of the 2005 Heisman Trophy
(Oklahoma).

Santonio Holmes
MVP of the 2008 Super Bowl.

Snap
The handing of the ball to the QUARTERBACK through the legs of the CENTER.

Steve Young
NFL Super Bowl MVP in 1994.

T. D. (Touchdown)
See TOUCHDOWN.

Tackle
In football, stopping another player by seizing him and bringing him to the ground; the players positioned between the guard and the end.

Terrell Davis
NFL Super Bowl MVP in 1997.

Tim Brown
1987 winner of the Heisman Trophy (Notre Dame).

Tim Tebow
Winner of the 2007 Heisman Trophy (Florida).

Tom Brady
MVP of the 2001 and 2003 Super Bowls.

Tom Landry
Former coach of the Dallas Cowboys.

Tony Dorsett
1976 Heisman Trophy winner (Pittsburgh).

Touchback
Touching the ball to the ground behind one's own goal line, the ball having been impelled over the goal line by an opponent.

Touchdown
Scoring six points.

Troy Aikman
NFL Super Bowl MVP in 1992.

Troy Smith
Winner of the 2006 Heisman Trophy (Ohio State).

Ty Detmer
1990 winner of the Heisman Trophy (Brigham Young University).

Vince Lombardi
Hall of Famer; coach of the Green Bay Packers and Washington Redskins from 1959 to 1970.

Vinny Testaverde
1986 winner of the Heisman Trophy (Miami).

Walter Payton
Former all-time NFL leader in rushing yards.

GOLF STARS AND TERMS

Allison Nicholas

Winner of the U.S. Women's Open in 1997.

Amy Alcott

1980 U.S. Women's Open Champion.

Annika Sorenstam

Winner of the 1995, 1996, and 2006 Women's Open.

Arnold Palmer

Winner of four Masters Tournaments, one U.S. Open, and two British Open Tournaments.

Ben Crenshaw

Won the Masters Tournament in 1995.

Ben Hogan

Winner of four U.S. Opens. In 1953, he won the Masters, the U.S. Open, and the British Open.

Bernhard Langer

Won the Masters Tournament in 1993.

Betsy King

Winner of the 1989 and 1990 U.S. Women's Open.

Birdie

A score of one under PAR.

Bogey

A score of one over PAR.

Bunker

A sand TRAP.

Corey Pavin

Won the U.S. Open in 1995.

Cristie Kerr

Winner 2007 U.S. Women's Open.

Davis Love III

Won the U.S. P.G.A. Championship in 1997.

Driver

The club normally used on the tee box for attaining distance.

Eagle

A score of two under PAR.

Ernie Els

Won the U.S. Open in 1994 and again in 1997. Also won British Open in 2002.

Fred Couples

Won the Masters Tournament in 1992.

Fuzzy Zoeller
Winner of the 1979 Masters and the 1984 U.S. Open.

Gary Player
1962 and 1972 P.G.A. Champion, winner of the 1965 U.S. Open, the 1961, 1974, and 1978 Masters, and the 1959, 1968, and 1974 British Open.

Greg Norman
Won the British Open in 1986 and 1993.

Hale Irwin
Won the U.S. Open in 1990.

Hazard
An obstacle on a golf course.

Hillary Lunke
Winner 2003 U.S. Women's Open.

Hollis Stacy
1977 and 1978 U.S. Women's Open champion.

Ian Baker-Finch
Won the British Open in 1991.

Ian Woosnam
Won the Masters Tournament in 1991.

Inbee Park
Winner 2008 U.S. Women's Open.

Jack Nicklaus
Winner of the following tournaments: six Masters, four U.S. Opens, five P.G.A.'s, and three British Opens.

Jan Stephenson
1983 U.S. Women's Open champion.

Jane Geddes
1986 U.S. Women's Open champion.

Janet Alex
1982 U.S. Women's Open champion.

John Daly
Won the U.S. P.G.A. in 1991, won the British Open in 1995.

Jose Maria Olazabal
Won the Masters Tournament in 1994 and again in 1999.

Julie Inkster
Winner of the 1999 and 2002 U.S. Women's Open.

Justin Leonard
Won the British Open in 1997.

Karrie Webb
Winner of the 2000 and 2001 U.S. Women's Open.

Kathy Baker
1985 U.S. Women's Open champion.

Laura Davies
1987 U.S. Women's Open champion.

Lauri Merten
Winner of the 1993 U.S. Women's Open.

Lee Janzen
Won the U.S. Open in 1993 and again in 1998.

Mark Brooks
Won the U.S. P.G.A. Championship in 1996.

Mark O'Meara
Won the Masters Tournament in 1996, won the British Open in 1998.

Meg Mallon
Winner of the 1991 U.S. Women's Open.

Mike Weir
Winner 2003 Masters.

Nick Faldo
Won the Masters Tournament in 1989, 1990, and again in 1996; also won the British Open in 1990 and 1992.

Nick Price
Won the U.S. P.G.A. Championship in 1994.

Par
The score standard for each of the holes on a golf course.

Pat Bradley
1981 U.S. Women's Open champion.

Patty Sheehan
Winner of the 1992 and 1994 U.S. Women's Open.

Paul Lawrie
Won the British Open in 1999.

Payne Stewart
Won the U.S. Open in 1991 and again in 1999, won the U.S. P.G.A. in 1989.

Phil Mickelson
Winner 2004 and 2006 U.S. Masters and the 2005 P.G.A. Championship.

Putter
The club used to hit the ball into the cup on the green.

Se Ri Pak
Winner of the 1998 U.S. Women's Open.

Steve Elkington
Won the U.S. P.G.A. in 1999.

Sports

Tiger Woods

Has won 14 major gold tournaments from 1997–2008. His achievements to date rank him among the most successful golfers of all time.

Tom Kite

Won the U.S. Open in 1992.

Tom Lehman

Won the British Open in 1996.

Trap

An area filled with sand to serve as a hazard.

Trevor Immelman

Winner 2008 U.S. Masters.

Vijay Singh

Won the Masters Tournament in 2000, won the U.S. P.G.A. Championship in 1998.

Wayne Grady

Won the U.S. P.G.A. Championship in 1990.

Wedge

A club with the head positioned at a large angle to allow for loft when the ball is hit.

Zach Johnson

Winner 2007 U.S. Masters.

"Tiger Woods"

HOCKEY STARS AND TERMS

Alexander Ovechkin

Winner of the 2007–2008 Hart Trophy-MVP.

Bobby Hull

Player, elected to the Hall of Fame, having spent the most productive years with the Chicago Blackhawks.

Brett Hull

Won the Hart Trophy-MVP in 1991 (St. Louis).

Chris Pronger

Won the Hart Trophy-MVP in 2000 (St. Louis).

Dominik Hasek

Won the Hart Trophy-MVP in 1997, and again in 1998 (Buffalo).

Eric Lindros

Won the Hart Trophy-MVP in 1995 (Philadelphia).

Goal

The net into which players try to advance a PUCK. In basketball, the HOOP into which players throw a ball.

Goalie

The player who defends the GOAL.

Gordie Howe

Won the Hart Trophy-MVP in 1952, 1953, 1957, 1958, 1960, and again in 1963 (Detroit).

Jaromir Jagr

Won the Hart Trophy-MVP in 1999 (Pittsburgh).

Joe Sakic

Winner of the 2000–2001 Hart Trophy-MVP.

Joe Thornton

Winner of the 2005–2006 Hart Trophy-MVP.

Jose Theodore

Winner of the 2001–2002 Hart Trophy-MVP.

Ken Daneyko

Winner of the Bill Masterson Trophy in 2000. He played for the New Jersey Devils (Perseverance, Sportsmanship, and Dedication to Hockey Award).

Mario Lemieux

Won the Hart Trophy-MVP in 1992, and again in 1996 (Pittsburgh).

Mark Messier

Won the Hart Trophy-MVP in 1990 (Edmonton), and in 1992 (New York Rangers).

Martin St. Louis

Winner of the 2003–2004 Hart Trophy-MVP.

Peter Forsberg

Winner of the 2002–2003 Hart Trophy-MVP.

Puck

The hard rubber disc used in play instead of a ball.

Sports

Sergei Fedorov
Won the Hart Trophy-MVP in 1994 (Detroit).

Sidney Crosby
Winner of the 2006-2007 Hart Trophy-MVP.

Steve Yzerman
Winner of the 2002 Frank Selke Trophy (Top Defensive Forward Award), for his play with the Detroit Red Wings.

SCHOOL AND COLLEGE MASCOTS AND NICKNAMES

Aggie	Charger	Nittany Lion	Reville
Bearcat	Demon	Jasper	Seminole
Bevo	Devil	Pacer	Sooner
Big Al	Gator	Panther	Spartan
Bomber	Grizzly	Racer	Titan
Blazer	Hoosier	Rambler	Trojan
Bruin	Horned Toad	Razorback	Viking
Buckeye	Husky	Red Raider	Wahoo
Cadet	Ichabod	Rocket	

TENNIS STARS AND TERMS

Ace
An unreturnable serve.

Andre Agassi
Won Wimbledon in 1992, and was the U.S. Open Champion in 1994 and 1999.

Billie Jean King
Winner of several indoor, U.S. Open, and Wimbledon titles (among others) during the 1960s and 1970s.

Bjorn Borg
One of the greatest players in the sport's history. He won 11 Grand Slam singles titles between 1974 and 1981.

Boris Becker
Three-time winner of Wimbledon (1985, 1986, and 1989) and winner of the U.S. Open (1989).

Chris Evert
Winner of several indoor, U.S. Open, and Wimbledon titles (among others) during the 1970s and 1980s.

Evonne Goolagong
Winner at Wimbledon in 1971 and 1980.

Jana Novotna
Won the Women's Wimbledon Championship in 1998.

Lindsay Davenport
Won the Women's U.S. Open Championship in 1998 and the Wimbledon Championship in 1999.

Marat Safin
Won the Men's U.S. Open in 2000.

Maria Sharapova
Winner of three Grand Slam singles titles, including the Women's Wimbledon at the age of 17 in 2004.

Martina Hingis
Won the Women's U.S. Open and Wimbledon in 1997.

Martina Navratilova
Winner of several indoor, U.S. Open, and Wimbledon titles during the late 1970s and 1980s.

Monica Seles
Winner of the U.S. Open in 1991 and 1992, and the 1993 and 1996 Australian Open.

Pancho Gonzales
Player who dominated the pro tour from 1953 to 1962.

Sports

Patrick Rafter

Won the U.S. Open Championship in 1997 and 1998.

Pete Sampras

Won the U.S. Open Championship in 1990, 1993, 1995, 1996, and 2002. Also won the Wimbledon Championship in 1993–1995 and 1997–2000.

Richard Krajicek

Won Wimbledon in 1996.

Serena Williams

Has won numerous major tennis tournaments including the Women's Wimbledon, the Women's Wimbledon Doubles, and the Women's U.S. Open.

Stefan Edberg

Won the U.S. Open Championship in 1991 and 1992.

Steffi Graf

Winner of several U.S. Open, Indoor, and Wimbledon titles during the 1980s and 1990s.

Venus Williams

Has won numerous major tennis tournaments including the Women's Wimbledon, the Women's Wimbledon Doubles, and the Women's U.S. Open.

MORE SPORTS IDEAS

Adidas

A brand of athletic wear.

Bobby Unser

Auto Racing: One of IndyCar's top twenty drivers.

Boxer

In boxing, one who fights with his fists.

Carl Lewis

Track and Field: World record holder in the 100-Meter Dash and the 200-Meter Dash (1984 Summer Olympic Games).

Cassius Clay

See MUHAMMAD ALI.

Dale Earnhardt

Auto Racing: Won the Winston Cup Championship 7 times, winning his last Championship in 1994.

Featherweight

In boxing, a BOXER weighing between 118 and 127 pounds.

Florence Griffith Joyner

Track and Field: 1988 Olympic gold medalist.

Floyd Patterson

Boxing: World HEAVYWEIGHT champion, 1956 to 1959, 1960 to 1962.

Flyweight

In boxing, a BOXER in the lightest weight class (weighing 112 pounds or less).

Frisbee

A brand of toy that resembles a "flying saucer."

George Foreman

Boxing: World HEAVYWEIGHT champion, 1970 to 1973.

Gutter

In bowling, the area on either side of the lane.

Heavyweight

In boxing, the class of BOXERS in the heaviest weight class, weighing over 175 pounds.

Hobie Cat

A brand of sailboat.

Jack Dempsey

Boxing: World HEAVYWEIGHT champion, 1919 to 1926.

Jackie Joyner-Kersee

Track and Field: 1988 Olympic goal medalist.

Jesse Owens

Track and Field: Winner of four Olympic gold medals in 1936.

Jim Thorpe

Pentathlon and Decathlon: 1912 Olympics in Stockholm, Sweden.

Joe Frazier

Boxing: World HEAVYWEIGHT champion, 1970 to 1973.

Joe Louis

Boxing: World HEAVYWEIGHT champion from 1937 to 1950.

KO (Knockout)

In boxing, defeating an opponent by causing him to fall onto the canvas and remain there for a count of ten.

Lightweight

In boxing, a BOXER weighing between 127 and 135 pounds.

Lob

In basketball, volleyball, and tennis, a shot that attains greater height than normal.

Michael Phelps

Winner of 8 Gold Medals in swimming in the 2008 Olympics in Beijing.

Michael Spinks

Boxing: World HEAVYWEIGHT champion, 1985 to 1986.

Middleweight
In boxing, a BOXER weighing between 148 and 160 pounds.

Muhammad Ali
Boxing: World HEAVYWEIGHT champion, 1964 to 1967; 1974 to 1978; and 1978 to 1979.

Nerf
A brand of toy.

Net
In tennis and volleyball, the barrier of meshwork cord that divides the playing field; also, in basketball, the cord under the rim on the backboard.

Nike
A brand of sportswear/shoes.

O.B.
"Out of bounds": In football and certain other games, the term applies to a ball out of play.

Olin
A brand of snow ski.

Pele
Soccer: Perhaps the most famous soccer player of all time. A Brazilian by birth, he made headlines in the 1960s and 1970s by his performances in the World Cup competition and retired in 1977.

Penalty
A loss of advantage enforced on a player or team for infraction of a rule.

Polo
A game played by people on horseback, using a wooden mallet to hit a wooden ball.

Randy Matson
Track and field: The Texas A&M shotputter who broke the world record in 1967; he won an Olympic gold medal the following year.

Reebok
A brand of sportswear/shoes.

Referee (Ref)
The official who enforces the rules in sports games.

Rocky Marciano
World HEAVYWEIGHT champion, 1952 to 1956.

Rookie
A player in his or her first year.

Rugby
A British game that has similarities to American football, basketball, soccer, and hockey.

Scrimmage
A team's practice session.

Server

In tennis, volleyball, and certain other games, the player who brings the ball into play.

Shotgun

A gun that fires multiple pellets through a smooth bore.

Skeet

A sport in which clay targets are thrown into the air and fired at from eight different stations.

Slingshot

A Y-shaped instrument with elastic bands attached; used for propelling objects.

Sonny Liston

Boxing: World HEAVYWEIGHT champion 1962 to 1964.

Spalding

A brand of sporting goods.

Spar

In boxing, going through the motions of boxing.

Spare

In bowling, knocking down all ten pins with two successive rolls of the ball.

Speedo

Brand of swimwear.

Spoon

Giving the ball an upward movement in certain games.

T.K.O.

Boxing: Technical knockout. This occurs when a match is ended because one of the boxers is unable to continue fighting, but has not been knocked down and counted out by the referee.

Umpire (Ump)

A person designated to rule on various plays, especially in baseball.

Volley

In tennis and volleyball, a series of successive returns of the ball from one side to the other.

Welterweight

In boxing, a BOXER who weighs between 136 and 147 pounds.

Wilson

Brand of sports equipment.

"Harley"

17

Transportation

Attention ladies and gentlemen, Flight 524 is now boarding at Gate 3. If you need assistance, please ask your flight attendant for suggestions.

Should you be traveling by car, watch for "Alfa Romeo" and "Ferrari"—they're fast and sometimes difficult to see.

Guarantee your reservation by selecting one of the choices in this chapter. (Cancellations must be made prior to 6 P.M. the day of your pet's arrival.)

How About . . .

Dodge   Mack

Eclipse   Scooter

Harley   Taxi

Jet

Transportation

Accord
An automobile made by Honda.

Acura
A luxury automobile made by Honda.

Alfa Romeo
An Italian sports car.

Altima
A mid-sized NISSAN sedan.

Amtrak
American Travel Track; railroad with the most extensive passenger service in the United States; created in 1970.

Audi
German-made automobile.

B-52
A bomber formerly made by BOEING for the U.S. Air Force, extensively used in aerial bombing.

Bentley
A luxury automobile made by ROLLS ROYCE.

Blazer
A recreational vehicle made by Chevrolet.

BMW (Beemer)
A German-made luxury automobile.

Boeing
An aircraft manufacturer.

Boxcar
A fully enclosed freight car.

Bronco
A recreational vehicle made by FORD.

Bugatti
An Italian sports car.

Buggy
A light, horse-drawn carriage.

Buick
An automobile made by General Motors.

Bus
A large passenger vehicle; also sometimes applied to an old car.

Cadillac
A luxury automobile made by General Motors.

Celica
A sports car made by TOYOTA.

Chevy

Chevrolet: an automobile made by General Motors.

Chrysler

An American automobile/manufacturer.

Corvette

A sports car made by Chevrolet. (See CHEVY.)

DeLorean

An automobile designed and manufactured by John DeLorean in the early 1980s in Belfast, Northern Ireland.

DeSoto

An automobile formerly made by CHRYSLER.

Diesel

Type of internal combustion engine, named for a German engineer.

Dodge

An automobile made by CHRYSLER.

Eclipse

A popular MITSUBISHI sports car.

Edsel

An automobile formerly made by FORD.

El Camino

The half-car, half-truck hybrid created by CHEVROLET.

Enola Gay

The name of the bomber used to deploy the first atomic bomb on Hiroshima, Japan.

Escalade

A luxurious S.U.V. manufactured by CADILLAC.

Ferrari

An Italian sports car.

Ford

An American automobile/manufacturer.

Harley

An American-made motocycle manufactured by Harley-Davidson, Inc.

Helicopter (Chopper)

An aircraft powered by a rotor.

Honda

A Japanese automobile/manufacturer.

Hovercraft

A personal transportation device consisting of a flying skateboard from the film *Back to the Future*.

"Edsel"

Hummer
The popular S.U.V. manufactured by GMC.

Jaguar
A British luxury automobile.

Jalopy
Run-down or outdated vehicle (usually a car).

Jeep
An American "general purpose vehicle."

Jet
A type of aircraft engine that propels an aircraft forward by expelling exhaust gases rearward.

Jetta
The VOLKSWAGEN sports coupe.

Lamborghini
Expensive Italian automobile.

Lexus
Japanese automobile.

Limo
Short for "limousine."

Lincoln
American automobile made by FORD.

Lotus
British automobile; no longer manufactured.

Mack
The sturdy, chrome-plated bulldog that stands atop the hood of all Mack trucks.

Mazda
A Japanese automobile/manufacturer.

Mercedes
A German luxury automobile manufactured by Mercedes Benz.

MG
A British sports car.

Microbus
The rectangular van popularized by VOLKSWAGEN.

Mitsubishi
A Japanese automobile/manufacturer.

Nissan
A Japanese automobile/manufacturer.

Panzer
A German tank used extensively in World War II.

Peugeot
A French automobile/manufacturer.

Piper
An American aircraft.

Polaris
An American manufacturer of off-road vehicles.

Porsche
A German sports car.

Prelude
An automobile made by HONDA.

Rambler
An automobile manufactured in the United States; it is no longer in production.

Regal
An automobile made by BUICK.

Rickshaw
A light carriage usually pulled by a bicycle or a person.

Rolls Royce
A British luxury automobile/manufacturer.

S.U.V.
The acronym for "Sport Utility Vehicle."

Saturn
Four-cylinder Pontiac automobile.

Schooner
A sailing vessel with two or more masts.

Scooter
A small, motorized, two-wheel vehicle.

Segway
A personal transportation device invented by Dean Kamen.

Seville
A luxury automobile made by CADILLAC.

RIDING IN STYLE . . .	
Alfa Romeo	**Lamborghini**
Audi	**Lexus**
Bentley	**Limo**
BMW	**Mercedes**
Cadillac	**Porche**
Escalade	**Rolls Royce**
Hummer	

Steamer
An early, steam-powered automobile.

Sterling
A British automobile/manufacturer.

Subaru
A Japanese automobile/manufacturer.

Suzuki
A Japanese automobile/manufacturer.

Taxi
A for-hire type of transportation.

T-Bird
Thunderbird: automobile made by FORD.

Toyota
A Japanese automobile/manufacturer.

Triumph
A British sports car.

Viper
A sports car made by DODGE.

Volkswagen
A German automobile/manufacturer.

Volvo
Swedish automobile.

Yamaha
A Japanese motorcycle/manufacturer.

"Astronaut"

18

Nature, Science, and Technology

Take a look at the world of possibilities here. You very well may have a "Gamma" or a "Tiger Lily" just waiting to have the proper title bestowed upon him or her.

How About . . .

Android	June Bug
Asteroid	Mars
Badger	Nessie
Daisy	Raven
Echo	Silk

Nature and Science

A. C.

Acacia

Acorn

Agate

Alfalfa

Amino

Android

Anion

Anode

Ape

Apollo

Argon

Ariel

Ash

Ashes

Aspen

Aster

Asteroid

Astro

Aurora

Autumn

Avalanche

Axis

Azalea

Badger

Bear

Beaver

Beetle

Begonia

Bengal

Beta

Blizzard

Blossom

Bluebonnet

Boa

Bobcat

Buck

Buckeye

Buckwheat

Buffalo

Bull

Bunny

Buttercup

Butterfly

Byte

Cactus

Calf

Canis Major

Caracal

Carnation

Cat

Catfish

Cathode

Cation

Cheetah

Chick

TOP OF THE FOOD CHAIN . . .	
Bear	Jaguar
Bengal	Leopard, Lion
Boa	Panther
Bobcat	Shark
Cheetah	Tiger
Gorilla	Whale
Grizzly	Wolf
Hawk	

Cloud	Delta	Foxfire	Honeysuckle
Cobra	Diamond	Foxtail	Hormone
Columbine	Dog	Foxy	Horse
Comet	Dove	Frog	Ice
Coot	Dynamite	Fungus	Iguana
Coral	Eagle	Galaxy	iPod
Corona	Earth	Gamma	Iris
Cosmos	Echo	Garden	Ivy
Cotton	Eclipse	'Gator	Jade
Coyote	Equinox	Geiser	Jaguar
Crab	Evening	Goat	Jaguarundi
Cricket	Feather	Goose	Jasmine
Cub	Felis	Grizzly	June Bug
Cyclone	Fern	Halley's Comet	Jupiter
Cypress	Fish	Halo	Kaffir
D. C.	Fission	Hawk	Kingfish
Daffodil	Flint	Hog	Krypton
Daisy	Flower	Holly	Larkspur
Dandelion	Fox	Honey Bee	Laser

Lava	Lynx	Mink	Orbit
Leech	Magneto	Mirage	Orchid
Leopard	Magnolia	Monkey	Ozone
Lightning	Marigold	Moon	Panda
Lilac	Mars	Morning Glory	Pansy
Lily	Meadow	Mule	Panther
Lion	Meerkat	Nebula	Parasite
Lizard	Megabyte	Neon	Petunia
Llama	Mercury	Neptune	Pig
Lotus	Micro	Nessie (Loch Ness Monster)	Pigeon
Lunar	Micron	Newt	Piranha
		Nocturne	Pluto
		Nova	Polar
		Nugget	Poppy
		Nuke	Primrose
		Ocelot	Puma
		Oleander	R.E.M.
		Onyx	Rabbit
			Radar

"Lizard"

Radon

Rainbow

Raven

Ripple

Rose

Rosebud

Ruby

Sage

Sagebrush

Sassafras

Saturn

Seismis

Serval

Shark

Sierra

Sigma

Silk

Silver

Skunk

Sky

Smoke

Snake

Snapdragon

Solar

Spider

Squirrel

Star

Steroids ("Roids")

Storm

Sun

Sunset

Sunshine

Sunspot

Supernova

Thor (rocket)

Thunder

Tiger

Tiger Lily

Toad

Topaz

Tornado

Tree

Tropical

Tulip

Tumbleweed

Turbo

Turkey

Turtle

Twilight

Uranus

Ursa Minor

Venus

Weasel

Weed

Whale

Wildcat

Willow

Wolf

Worm

X ray

Zebra

Zinnia

STORMS AND DISASTERS . . .	
Avalanche	Lightning
Blizzard	Thunder
Cyclone	Tornado
Earthquake	Tsunami
Hurricane	

"Donut"

19

Foods

In every veterinarian's files, you will find many pets named after foods—from "Bagel" and "Biscuit" to "Taffy" and "Truffle." For a perfectly delicious sampling of names, take a look at this chapter of culinary delights.

How About . . .

Apple

Blackberry

Brownie

Candy

Cheeto

Cinnamon

Egg Roll

Honey

Peanut

Shrimp

Waffle

Foods

Anchovy

Angel Food

Apple

Asparagus

Avocado

Baby Ruth (a brand of candy bar)

Bagel

Banana

Basil

Beef

Berry

Biscuit

Blackberry

Blueberry

Bosco (a brand of chocolate syrup)

Brie (a cheese)

Bromley (a type of apple)

Brownie

Bubble Gum

Butter

Buttercup

Butterfingers (a brand of chocolate candy bar)

Buttermilk

Candy

Caramel

Carrot

Cashew

Casserole

Caviar

Chalupa (a type of Mexican food consisting of a flat fried tortilla topped with refried beans and cheese)

Cheddar

Cheerio (a brand of breakfast cereal)

Cheeseburger

Cheesecake

Cheeto (a brand of snack chip)

Cherry

Chestnut

Chicken

Chili

Chip(s)

Chiquita (a brand of bananas)

Chocolate

Chocolate Chip

Chung King (a brand of Chinese food)

Cinnamon

Cinnamon Muffin

Clove

Cocoa

Coconut

Coffee

Cookie

Crackerjack

Crackers

Crepe (a thin pancake)

Crisco (a brand of shortening)

Croissant

Crouton

Cupcake

Curry (a mixture of spices used in Indian cooking)

Custard

Divinity (Fudge)

Donut

Dorito (a brand of corn chip)

Egg Roll

Eggplant

Enchilada (a type of Mexican food consisting of a tortilla filled with meat or cheese)

Escargot (a French delicacy of snails prepared in butter, parsley, and garlic)

Fajita (a type of Mexican food consisting of strips of barbecued meat, usually beef or chicken, served with TORTILLAS)

Frankfurter

MEATS . . .	
Beef	Pork Chop
Cheeseburger	Sausage
Chicken	Shrimp
Escargot	Sushi
Frankfurter	T-Bone
Ham	Tenderloin
Meatball	Weiner

Foods

French Fry

Frito (a brand of corn chip)

Fruit Loop (a brand of cereal)

Fudge

Garbanzo (a type of plant with an edible seed)

Ginger

Ginger Snap

Ginseng

Gravy

Grits

Guacamole (mashed and seasoned avacado)

Gum Drop

Gummi Bear (a brand of candy)

Häagen Dazs (a brand of ice cream)

Ham

Hershey (a brand of chocolate)

Honey

Hormel (a brand of meat products)

Hot Dog

Hydrox (a brand of cookies)

Jalapeno (a type of hot pepper)

Jambalaya (a Cajun dish)

Java

Jello

Jelly

Jelly Bean

Jerky (a dried beef snack)

Kibble (a type of dry dog food)

Kiwi

Kuchen (a German coffee cake with a shortbread crust)

Kumquat (a type of citrus fruit)

Lemon

Lemon Drop

Licorice

Lime

Linguini

Lollipop

Macaroni

Mango

Marshmallow

Meat

Meatball

Meringue (stiffly beaten egg whites and sugar used as a dessert topping)

Molasses

Monterey Jack (a type of cheese)

Muffin

Mushroom

Mustard

Nacho (a type of Mexican food consisting of a chip topped with refried beans, cheese, and/or jalapeño peppers)

Noodle

Nutmeg

O. J. (orange juice)

Oatmeal

Olive

Onion

Orange

Oreo (a brand of cookie)

Oscar Mayer (a brand of meat products)

Pancake

Paprika

Peaches

Peanut(s)

Pepper

Pepper Shaker

Peppermint

Perugina (dark brown chocolate)

Phyllo (paper-thin sheets of pastry used in the preparation of Greek desserts and appetizers)

Pickles

Pinto

Pistachio

Pizza

Popsicle

Popcorn

Pork Chop

Potato

Pretzel

Pringle

Pudding

Pumpernickel

Pumpkin

Quiche

Raisin

Raisin Bran

Raspberry

Relish

Rhubarb

Ribeye

Ritz (a brand of cracker)

Sage

Salt

Sassafras (a type of tea)

Sauce

Sausage

Schnitzel

Sesame

Shortcake

Shrimp

Sirloin

Skippy (a brand of peanut butter)

Smuckers (a brand of jams and jellies)

Snickers (a brand of candy bar)

Soda

Souffle

Soup

Spaghetti

Spearmint

Spice

Spicey

Spud (Potato)

Squash

Strawberry

Strudel

Sugar

Sundae

Sushi (a type of Japanese food consisting of raw fish and seasoned rice)

Syrup

T-Bone

Tabasco (a brand of hot sauce)

Taco (a type of Mexican food consisting of a folded tortilla filled with meat, cheese, and spices)

Taffy

Tamale (a type of Mexican food consisting of minced meat and spices rolled in a corn dough and cooked in the wrapping of a corn husk)

Tangerine

Tapioca Pudding

Tater (potato)

Tenderloin

Tiramisu (an Italian dessert)

Toffee (a hard or chewy candy)

Tofu

Tomato

Tootsie Roll

Tortilla (a type of Mexican food consisting of a thin baked circular piece of dough, the main ingredient being corn or flour)

Truffle

Turnip

Twinkie (a brand of snack cake)

Vanilla

Vichyssoise

Waffle

Weiner

Wheaties (a brand of breakfast cereal)

Wishbone

Ziplock (a brand of food storage bags)

FRUITS & VEGETABLES . . .	
Apple	Cherry
Asparagus	Eggplant
Banana	Grapes
Blackberry	Raisin
Blueberry	Squash
Carrot	

"Brandy"

Liquors and Drinks

20

Belly up to the bar. . . . Undoubtedly, some of the following names were selected after the pet owners did just that. (Not all the drinks listed are alcoholic).

Cheers to you and your new pet!

How About . . .

Amaretto	Martini
Budweiser	Tequila
Jack Daniels	Vodka
Kamikaze	Zinfandel

Liquors and Drinks

Amaretto
Almond LIQUEUR.

Amstel
A brand of beer.

Asahi
A brand of Japanese beer.

Asti
Asti Spumante.

Bahama Mama
A cocktail.

Bartles (Bartles and Jaymes)
A brand of wine cooler.

Beaujolais
A type of red wine.

Beaulieu
A California winery.

Beck's
A brand of German beer.

Big Red
A brand of soft drink.

Bordeaux
A type of red wine.

Bourbon
A liquor distilled from a mash of corn, rye, and malted barley.

Brandy
A liquor distilled from fermented grapes or other fruit.

Budweiser
A brand of American beer.

Cabernet (Sauvignon)
A type of red wine.

Canadian Club (C. C.)
A brand of Canadian WHISKEY.

Cappucino
A drink made with strong coffee and hot milk.

Celis
A brand of beer.

WINES . . .	
Beaujolais	**Chablis**
Cabernet	**Merlot**
Chardonnay	**Sebastiani**
Claret	**Spatlese**
Chianti	**Verdillac**
Champagne	**Zinfandel**

Chablis
A type of white wine.

Chai
A type of tea.

Champagne
An effervescent wine.

Chardonnay
A type of white wine.

Chianti
An Italian red wine.

Chivas (Regal)
A brand of Scotch WHISKEY.

Claret
A type of red wine.

Coca-Cola (Coke)
A brand of soft drink.

Cocoa
A beverage made from the defatted portion of the cocoa bean.

Coffee
A beverage made from roasted and ground coffee beans.

Cognac
A type of French BRANDY.

Coors
An American beer.

Corona
A brand of Mexican beer.

Courvoisier
A brand of French COGNAC.

Cuervo
A brand of Mexican TEQUILA.

Daiquiri
A frozen or iced drink made with fruit juice, sugar, and rum.

Dewars
A brand of Scotch WHISKEY.

Dixie
A brand of American beer.

Dos Equis
A brand of Mexican beer.

Dr. Pepper
A brand of soft drink.

Foster's
A brand of beer.

Gin
A liquor flavored with juniper berries.

Glen Ellen
A brand of wine.

Grolsch
A brand of Dutch beer.

Harvey Wallbanger
A cocktail.

Heineken
A brand of Dutch beer.

Hurricane
A cocktail.

Jack Daniels
A brand of Tennesee WHISKEY.

Jax
A brand of American beer.

Jaymes (Bartles and Jaymes)
A brand of wine cooler.

Jigger(s)
A measure used in making mixed drinks (usually 1¹/₂ ounces).

Kahlúa
A brand of Mexican coffee liqueur.

Kamikaze
A cocktail.

Killian('s)
A brand of American beer.

Kirin
A brand of Japanese beer.

Lemonade
A beverage made with lemon juice, sugar, and water.

Liqueur
A sweetened, flavored liquor.

Mai Tai
A cocktail.

Margarita
A cocktail.

Martini
A cocktail.

Merlot
A type of red wine.

Miller
A brand of American beer.

Mint Julep
A cocktail.

Mocha
A rich Arabian coffee; a drink made by mixing coffee with chocolate.

Molson
A brand of Canadian beer.

Moosehead
A brand of Canadian beer.

Moretti
A brand of Italian beer.

Mr. Pibb
A brand of soft drink.

Napa
A valley in California where grapes are grown to make wine.

Nehi
A brand of soft drink.

Old Milwaukee
A brand of American beer.

Pabst (Blue Ribbon)
A brand of American beer.

Pacifico
A brand of beer.

Pearl
A brand of Texas beer.

Pepe Lopez
A brand of Mexican TEQUILA.

Pepsi
A brand of soft drink.

Peroni
A brand of Italian beer.

R. C. Cola
A brand of soft drink.

Red Dog
A brand of beer.

Red Stripe
A brand of beer.

Root Beer
A soft drink.

COCKTAILS . . .	
Amaretto Sour	**Margarita**
Bahama Mama	**Martini**
Bazooka	**Mint Julep**
Harvey Wallbanger	**Screwdriver**
Kamikaze	**Singapore Sling**
Madras	**Sprizter**
Mai Tai	**Swizzle**

Liquors and Drinks

Sake
A Japanese alcoholic beverage made from rice.

Samuel Adams
A brand of American beer.

Samuel Smith('s)
A brand of British beer.

Sapporo
A brand of Japanese beer.

Schnapps
Various flavored LIQUEURS.

Scotch
A WHISKEY distilled from malted barley.

Seagram's
A brand of American blended WHISKEY.

Sebastiani
A California wine/winery.

Seven Up
A brand of soft drink.

Shasta
A brand of soft drink.

Shiner Bock
A brand of beer.

Singapore Sling
A cocktail.

Slice
A brand of soft drink.

Soda
A flavored soft drink; unflavored carbonated water; a mixture of the latter with ice cream and syrup.

Soda Pop
A flavored soft drink.

Spatlese
A type of German white wine.

Sprite
A brand of soft drink.

Spritzer
A cocktail.

St. Pauli Girl
A brand of German beer.

Starbucks
A brand of coffee.

Stolychnaya (Stoli)
A brand of Russian VODKA.

Stroh's
A brand of American beer.

Superior
A brand of Mexican beer.

Swizzle
A cocktail.

Tea
A beverage brewed from the leaves of the tea plant.

Tecate
A brand of Mexican beer.

Tequila
A liquor distilled from mescal.

Tonic
Anything that refreshes or rejuvenates; a regional carbonated water.

Tucher Weiss
A brand of beer.

Two Fingers
A brand of Mexican TEQUILA.

Verdillac
A French wine.

Vodka
A colorless, "neutral" liquor distilled from grain.

Watney's
A brand of British beer.

Whiskey
Any liquor distilled from a grain mash.

Wild Turkey
A brand of Kentucky WHISKEY.

Xing Tao
A brand of Chinese beer.

Zima
A brand of American beer.

Zinfandel
A red, white, or blush wine made from California's Zinfandel grape.

"L.L. Bean"

21

Fashion

You don't have to be a devotee of design to consider some of the names in this chapter. The right name for your fashionable pet might be close at hand . . . or on your feet!

How About . . .

Argyle

Carrie Bradshaw

Cashmere

Coco Chanel

Dior

Elle

Fendi

Louboutin

Onyx

Pearl

Prada

UGG

Vogue

Argyle
A pattern consisting of diamonds in diagonal checkerboard arrangement.

Bergdorf Goodman
Upscale department store in Manhattan.

Billabong
A brand of surfer clothing.

Blue Jean
Pants or trousers, usually made from denim.

Burberry
A British luxury fashion house that manufactures clothing and fashion accessories. They are widely known for their signature tartan plaid.

Calvin Klein
Designer; brand of clothing.

Carolina Herrera
A brand of fragrance named for the designer.

Carrie Bradshaw
Sarah Jessica Parker's character in *Sex & the City*.

Cashmere
A fine woolen fabric made from the hair of the kashmir goat.

Chaps
Protective leather leg coverings worn by cowboys. Also a brand of cologne.

Chic
A brand of clothing; highly fashionable.

Chloë
A brand of fragrance.

Christian Dior
Designer; brand of clothing; fragrance and cosmetics.

Coco Chanel
A French designer, brand of clothing, and fragrance.

Cosmopolitan
An International magazine for women, also known as "Cosmo."

Coach
An American brand of leather goods and clothing.

Cotton
A soft, staple fiber.

Couture (Haute Couture)
Refers to the creation of exclusive custom-fitted clothing.

Denim
A type of rugged cotton twill textile.

Diamond
A precious stone.

Dior (Christian Dior)
A French high-fashion clothing retailer.

Dolce & Gabana
Commonly abbreviated at D & G, is an Italian luxury fashion house.

Dooney & Bourke
A company specializing in fashion accessories, particularly handbags and leather goods.

Elle
A fashion magazine.

Emerald
A precious stone.

Esprit
A brand of clothing.

Fendi
An Italian fashion house best known for its "baguette" handbags.

Gap
An American clothing and accessories retailer based in California.

"Dolce & Gabana"

Giorgio Armani

An Italian fashion designer.

Givenchy

A French brand of clothing, accessories, perfumes, and cosmetics.

Glamour

An American women's magazine originally called *Glamour of Hollywood*.

Gold

A precious metal, with yellow and pink tones, used in jewelry and ornamentation.

GQ

Men's fashion and lifestyle magazine.

Gucci

An iconic Italian fashion and leather goods label.

Harrod(s)

A department store located in London, England.

Hobo

A style of handbag or purse that is typically large and characterized by a crescent shape.

Hermes

A French high fashion house specializing in leather and clothing.

Hilfiger

Tommy Hilfiger is an American fashion designer.

Jade

A gemstone, usually pale green or white.

Jean-Paul Gaultier

A French haute couture fashion designer.

Juicy Couture

A contemporary line of both casual and dressy apparel based in California known for their terrycloth and velour tracksuits.

Kate Spade

The designer of "Kate Spade New York," known for her handbags.

L. L. Bean

A mail-order clothing company and brand of outdoor clothing products.

Lace

An openwork fabric, patterned with open holes in the work.

L.A.M.B.

A fashion line by American singer Gwen Stefani. It is an acronym for Love. Angel. Music. Baby.

Levi

A brand of sportswear.

Lipstick

A type of cosmetic used to heighten lip color.

Louboutin

Christian Louboutin is a French footwear designer and is known for his line of high-end women's shoes with signature red soles.

Lucky

A fashion magazine that calls itself the "Ultimate Shopping Guide." Also, "Lucky" Brand Jeans is a designer denim company in California.

Mademoiselle

Was an influential women's magazine published until 2001. Also, Madesmoiselle is the French-language equivalent of "Miss."

Mary Kate & Ashley

The Olsen twins are actresses and Fashionistas.

Missoni

An Italian fashion house famous for its unique knitwear, made from a variety of fabrics in colorful patterns.

Moschino

An Italian fashion design house.

Neiman Marcus

An American luxury specialty retail department store.

Onyx

A black gemstone used in jewelry.

Oscar de la Renta

One of the world's leading fashion designers.

Oxford

A style of shoe with laces; a type of cotton cloth.

Paisley

A multicolored pattern of curving shapes used to decorate fabric.

Pairs

A brand of fragrance.

Pearl

A lustrous concretion formed inside an oyster.

Plaid
A patterned woolen cloth.

Platinum
A pure metal used for fine jewelry, platinum is silvery-white in appearance, and is more precious than silver and gold.

Polo
A brand of clothing designed by RALPH LAUREN.

Poncho
(1) A loose fitting piece of clothing worn by some Mexicans. (2) A garment made of plastic or other waterproof material, used as a raincoat.

Prada
Very successful fashion designer

Pret-a-porter
French equivalent of "ready to wear" or "off the rack."

Ralph Lauren
Designer; brand of clothing.

Rolex
A brand of wristwatch.

Roxy
A brand of clothing for surfing and skiing.

Ruby
A precious stone.

SAKS
"Saks Fifth Avenue" is a luxury American department store.

Sapphire
A precious stone.

Satin
A lustrous fabric made of silk or rayon.

Seiko
A brand of wristwatch from Japan.

Silver
A precious metal, with a white metallic luster, used in jewelry and coinage.

Sterling
Silver that is nearly pure (925 parts silver to 75 parts copper).

Tag (Heuer)
A Swiss luxury watch maker.

Tiara
A crown of jewels.

Tiffany
A fashionable jewelry store in New York City.

Topaz
A semi-precious stone.

Tux
Short for tuxedo—formal attire for a man.

UGG
A style and brand of Australian sheepskin boot.

Valentino
An Italian clothing company founded by Valentino Garavani.

Velvet
A fabric made of silk, rayon, etc., which has a soft, luxuriant texture.

Versace (Gianni and Donatella)
An Italian fashion label.

Vogue
An international fashion and lifestyle magazine.

Wrangler
A brand of clothing.

Yves Saint Laurent
A luxury fashion house.

"Max" and "Moritz"

22

Pairs

So you're having twice as much fun now that you have two little critters, right? Well, relax and enjoy it by taking a look at these interesting combinations. Perhaps you'll find that very special one-of-a-kind name for your very special two-of-a-kind friends.

How About . . .

ANTONY & CLEOPATRA

BARNEY & FRED

CAIN & ABEL

DUKE & DUCHESS

FRED & ETHEL

ROMEO & JULIET

SALT & PEPPER

WILBUR & CHARLOTTE

Abbott & Costello (See Chapter 11)

Adam & Eve (See Chapter 7)

Anion & Cation (See Chapter 18)

Anode & Cathode (See Chapter 18)

Antony & Cleopatra

Apples & Oranges

Aurora & Boring Alice (See Chapter 18)

Back & Forth

Barney & Fred (See Chapter 14)

Barnum & Bailey (See Chapter 5)

Baron & Baroness

Bartles & Jaymes

Baucis & Philemon (See Chapter 6)

Beavis & Butt-head (See Chapter 14)

Bert & Ernie (See Chapter 11)

Betty & Wilma (See Chapter 14)

Big & Bad

Biton & Cleobis (See Chapter 6)

Black & White

Bogey & Bacall (See Chapter 11)

Bonnie & Clyde

Briggs & Stratton (a type of engine)

Cagney & Lacey

Cain & Abel (See Chapter 7)

Calvin & Hobbes (See Chapter 14)

Carlos & Charlie (a restaurant in Mexico)

Castor & Pollux (See Chapter 6)

Chainsaw & Sawdust

Cheech & Chong (comedians)

Chips & Salsa

Chocolate & Vanilla

Count & Countess

Cupid & Psyche (See Chapter 6)

Czar & Czarina

David & Goliath (See Chapter 7)

Ding & Ling

Dagwood & Blondie (See Chapter 14)

Down & Out

Dr. Jekyll & Mr. Hyde

Dude & Dudette

Duke & Duchess

East & West

Ebony & Ivory

Elvis & Priscilla

Emperor & Empress

Felix & Oscar (See Chapter 11)

Ferdinand & Isabella (See Chapter 5)

First & Ten

Foot Loose & Fancy Free

Frank and Stein

Fred & Ethel (See Chapter 11)

George & Gracie

Get Off the Rug & You Too

Glimmer & Twynkle

Goodness & Mercy

Groucho & Harpo (See Chapter 15)

Happy & Sad

Harley & Davidson

Hera & Zeus (See Chapter 6)

Hero & Leander (See Chapter 6)

Him & Her (See Chapter 5)

Hollywood & Vine

Hoot & Holler

Hunkie & Dorie

Hunnies & Funnies

Itsy & Bitsy

King & Queen

Kit & Kaboodle

Kut & Kutta (See Chapter 9)

Lady & Tramp (See Chapter 11)

Laurel & Hardy (See Chapter 11)

Laverne & Shirley (See Chapter 11)

Licker & Whiner

Lord & Lady

Love 'Em & Leave 'Em

Lucy & Ricky (See Chapter 11)

Marco & Polo

Mason & Dixon

Max & Moritz (See Chapter 10)

Pairs

Mickey & Minnie (See Chapter 14)

Mutt & Jeff (See Chapter 14)

Napoleon & Josephine (See Chapter 5)

Nieman & Marcus (See Chapter 21)

Nip & Tuck

North & South

Now & Then

Null & Void

Orpheus & Eurydice (See Chapter 6)

Otis & Milo (See Chapter 11)

Ozzie & Harriet (See Chapter 11)

Patience & Fortitude (See Chapter 10)

Patriarch & Matriarch

Pete & Repeat

Ping & Pong

Porgy & Bess

"Salt & Pepper"

Prince & Princess

Prose & Kahn

Pyramus & Thisbe (See Chapter 6)

Ralph & Alice (See Chapter 11)

Regis & Kathie Lee

Ren & Stimpy (See Chapter 14)

Romeo & Juliet (See Chapter 10)

Rough & Ready

Ruff & Tuff

Salt & Pepper

Samson & Delilah (See Chapter 7)

Scarlett & Rhett (See Chapter 11)

Simon & Garfunkel

Simon & Schuster (See Chapter 10)

Sonny & Cher (See Chapter 15)

Stanley & Livingstone (See Chapter 5)

Starsky & Hutch (characters in T.V. series)

Sugar & Spice

Taco & Chalada (See Chapter 19)

Teeter & Totter

Thunder & Lightning

Tick & Tock

Tom & Jerry (See Chapter 14)

Topsy & Turvy

Venus & Adonis (See Chapter 10)

Waylon & Willy

When & If

Wilbur & Charlotte (See Chapter 10)

Wilbur & Orville (See Chapter 5)

"Larry, Moe, & Curly"

Trios

Here's a sampling of the endless possibilities for owners of three pets.

For additional ideas, consider the topics and names in Chapters 1–21; staying within a given category for all three names makes a more interesting combination.

One word of caution: Names that rhyme may sound confusing to animals. However, if they already seem confused, try Larry, Moe, and Curly.

Trios

"Good, Bad, & Ugly"

REGISTERING A NAME WITH THE AMERICAN KENNEL CLUB

If your dog will be registered by the American Kennel Club (AKC), you need to follow the guidelines established by the AKC:

The person who owns the dog and applies to register it has the right to name the dog. On registration applications issued starting in mid-1989 a space is provided for only one name choice. Registration applications issued prior to that time have spaces for two name choices. It is not necessary to indicate a second name choice, but if you do, consider both names carefully. There is always a chance that the second will be approved and, therefore, it should be equally desirable by the owner. A dog's name may not be changed after it is registered.

Name choices are limited to 25 letters.

No Arabic or Roman numerals may be included in name choices, and no written number is permitted at the end of names. AKC reserves the right to assign a Roman numeral. AKC permits thirty-seven dogs of each breed to be assigned the same name, and many common names such as Spot, Snoopy, Lassie, King, etc., are fully allotted. The shorter the name choice the greater the chances that AKC will assign a Roman numeral or that the name may not be accepted at all. The longer and more unique the name chosen, the greater the chance for approval. The easiest way to lengthen a name is to incorporate your surname, for example, "Smith's Spot" instead of Spot.

Remember that the dog's "call name," that is, the name he responds to, does not have to be the same as his registered name. If you name your dog "Spot" and it is not approved, you may continue to call him "Spot," even though his registered name may be different.

Incorrect spelling and grammar are not corrected by AKC. Names are approved as submitted. A change in spelling is considered a change of name and is not allowed.

Do not include:

1. Names of prominent people, living or recently deceased.
2. Words or abbreviations that imply AKC titles (Champ, Winner).
3. The words: Dog, Male, Sire, Bitch, Female, Dam, Kennel.
4. Words that are disparaging or obscene.
5. Roman or Arabic numerals.
6. Breed names alone.*

To obtain applications or more information concerning AKC registration and requirements, write to:

American Kennel Club
51 Madison Avenue
New York, New York 10010

*American Kennel Club, *Dogs, General Information* (New York: American Kennel Club), pp. 21–22. Used with permission.

Help me make *The Best Pet Name Book Ever* even better!

Just in case I forgot your favorite pet name, please send it to me so I can include it in the next edition of this book.

If there is a story or explanation behind your choice of name, please include that, too.

Send all nominations for the next edition to:

Wayne Bryant Eldridge
c/o Barron's Educational Series, Inc.
250 Wireless Boulevard
Hauppauge, NY 11788